Godard: Three Films

Also in this series:

MASTERWORKS OF THE GERMAN CINEMA

The Golem, Nosferatu, M, The Threepenny Opera

MASTERWORKS OF THE FRENCH CINEMA

The Italian Straw Hat, Grand Illusion,
La Ronde, The Wages of Fear

MASTERWORKS OF THE BRITISH CINEMA

Brief Encounter, The Third Man, Kind Hearts
and Coronets, Saturday Night and Sunday Morning

EISENSTEIN: THREE FILM SCRIPTS

Battleship Potemkin, October, Alexander Nevsky

POLANSKI: THREE FILM SCRIPTS

Knife in the Water, Repulsion, Cul-de-Sac

Godard: Three Films

Introduction by Alistair Whyte

A Woman is a Woman

A Married Woman

Two or Three Things I Know About Her

Icon Editions

Harper & Row, Publishers

New York, Evanston, San Francisco, London

4938080156

Original screenplays entitled:
Une femme est une femme (1961)
Une femme mariée (1964)
Deux ou trois choses que je sais d'elle (1966)
Copyright © Jean-Luc Godard 1967

Godard: Three Films Copyright © 1975 by Lorrimer Publishing Ltd.

FIRST US EDITION

ISBN: 0-06-438920-0 (cloth) 0-06-430065-X (paper)

LIBRARY OF CONGRESS CATALOG CARD NUMBER: 75-4352

CONTENTS

ACKNOWLEDGEMENTS

The publishers wish to thank the following individuals and organisations for their help in the preparation of this volume: the British Film Institute for the provision of viewing facilities; Studio Vista for permission to reprint an article on *A Woman is a Woman* and *Two or Three Things I Know About Her;* The Observer for permission to reprint an article on *A Married Woman;* Joel Finler for the loan of stills; Alistair Whyte for permission to reprint an interview with Anna Karina. *A Woman is a Woman, A Married Woman* and *Two or Three Things I Know About Her* were translated respectively by Jan Dawson, Susan Bennett and Marianne Alexander.

INTRODUCTION

by Alistair Whyte

Jean-Luc Godard made his first feature, *Breathless*, in 1959, the year in which the term '*nouvelle vague*' was coined by the press to describe the new currents in French cinema. Both François Truffaut's *Four Hundred Blows* and Alain Resnais' *Hiroshima, Mon Amour* had won prizes at the Cannes festival with the result that producers were keen to finance new film-makers in the hope of quick returns. Between 1959 and 1963 well over a hundred first features were made in France but, inevitably, most of these have sunk into oblivion. A handful of extremely talented directors did, however, emerge from the 'new wave' and Jean-Luc Godard is undoubtedly the most controversial of these. His films have been the object of both extreme adulation and vitriolic abuse: for Richard Roud, he is 'one of the most important artists of our time' while, for Raymond Durgnat, Godard 'wears dark glasses to hide from the world that he is in a permanent state of ocular masturbation, rubbing himself off against anything and everything on which his eye alights.'[1]

One of the two main reasons for such an acute divergence of opinion is Godard's rejection of cinematic conventions, or, what his detractors might call, his wilful obscurity. When he made *Breathless* he said he 'wanted to take a conventional story and remake, but differently, everything the cinema had done . . . to give the feeling that the techniques of film-making had been discovered for the first time.'[2] This statement reveals his ambition to reinvent the language of cinema, which is closely allied to a desire to make the medium of film, itself, a major topic of his work. For his first feature, Godard took the plot of a banal thriller but the downbeat relationships between the characters, and the 'breathless' pace of the film achieved by jump-cuts and the hand-held camera, created an elliptical work of extraordinary immediacy. In *Breathless*, as in all his subsequent films Godard ignores accepted norms of continuity, destroys the 'illusion of reality', and constantly reminds the spectator that he is watching a film.

7

The second major reason for the controversy surrounding Godard is the development of his social and political awareness, for which he was attacked not only by the Right but also by many Left-wing critics, who objected to his unconventional treatment of ' serious ' problems. Yet he was one of the few people who seemed to sense the latent violence under the surface calm of Gaullist France: in *La Chinoise*, made in 1967, he showed a group of militant, Left-wing students at Nanterre, willing to participate in direct revolutionary action. When the film appeared, it was dismissed as pure fantasy, but it proved to be uncannily prophetic. In May 1968 a series of student riots in Paris escalated into a mass uprising which threatened to overthrow the government. But the revolution was not at hand and the euphoria of the militants was short-lived. During the June elections, the Gaullists were returned to power with a greatly increased majority. For Godard, May 1968 was a turning-point: he committed himself to revolutionary action, declaring his intention to ' destroy cinema ' and its ' bourgeois concept of representation '. Until 1972, when he made *Tout va bien* with Jean-Pierre Gorin, it appeared that no new film from Godard would ever reach the normal avenues of distribution, and that he had abandoned as fruitless any dialogue with the middle-class cinema-goer.

Although they are unlikely to convert Godard's detractors, the three films presented in this volume are admirably suited for comparison and clearly illustrate both Godard's experiments with the language of cinema and his growing political commitment. *A Woman is a Woman* (*Une Femme est Une Femme*) (1961), *A Married Woman* (*Une Femme Mariée*) (1964), and *Two or Three Things I Know About Her* (*Deux ou Trois Choses que je sais d'elle*) (1966) form a trilogy in which the director, at different stages of his career, deals with twenty-four hours in the life of a woman living in Paris.

The first of these films is a nostalgic parody of a Hollywood musical, constructed around an amusing reworking of the eternal triangle. The characters in *A Woman is a Woman* act as if they are in a musical, but against the background of noisy Parisian cafés, genuine streets and seedy strip-clubs rather than stylised Hollywood sets. At one point Anna Karina says that she would like to be in a film choreographed by Bob Fosse, and there follows a sequence of rapid shots in which she and Jean-Paul Belmondo attempt, rather clumsily, to freeze in positions which a Cyd Charisse or a Gene Kelly would have held with effortless grace. There is an element of paradox here which is reinforced by the film's score. As Godard himself said, he tried ' to convey through music the idea that the characters are singing although they are speaking normally '. When, in fact, Angela does sing during her strip-routine, there is no accompaniment whatsoever, with the result that her voice sounds poignantly faint and rather flat. In *A Woman is a Woman* Godard has taken the Hollywood musical and turned it affectionately on its head.

All this may appear rather contradictory and disruptive, but Godard is fascinated by contradiction and is not concerned with making the spectator suspend his disbelief. Throughout *A Woman is a Woman* he uses numerous different devices: during the credits the noise of the film crew can be heard; from time to time the actors acknowledge the presence of the cinema audience; there are sudden changes of mood and absurd gags, such as the egg which Angela flips in the air and catches a few minutes later, after taking a telephone call; and there are many references to the cinema, not only to the Hollywood musical but to films by the ' new wave ' of directors. He refers to Truffaut's *Shoot the Piano Player* and *Jules and Jim* (with walk-on parts by the leading ladies, Marie Dubois and Jeanne Moreau), to Jacques Demy's *Lola*, and even to *Breathless*. The director constantly reminds the spectator that he is not watching life but a spectacle.

Allusions to the cinema, often heightening or underlining important themes and particular scenes, are a feature of all Godard's films. In *A Married Woman* there is again mention of *Lola;* a poster for Hitchcock's *Spellbound* can be glimpsed; and a snatch of the soundtrack of Alain Resnais' *Night and Fog* can be heard in the cinema at Orly, where Charlotte meets her lover. In *Two or Three Things I Know About Her,* which Godard himself described as ' a continuation of the movement begun by Resnais in *Muriel,* a poster for this film is prominently displayed. It must be remembered that, like many other ' *nouvelle vague* ' directors, Godard came to film-making via criticism; he was an ardent cinema-goer regularly attending the eclectic programmes of Henri Langlois' Cinematheque. The first ' new wave ' features were, in his own words, the ' work of film enthusiasts ', who imitated and adapted techniques they admired in other directors. Many shots and scenes in Godard's films are directly inspired by other people's work, especially Hollywood genre-movies. 'I thought in terms of purely cinematographic attitudes', he said in an interview of 1962. 'For some shots I referred to scenes I remembered from Preminger, Cukor, etc.'[3]

As Godard himself pointed out, these cinematic references can be compared to the literary quotations which abound in his films. In *A Woman is a Woman* there are lines from Alfred de Musset's *On ne badine pas avec l'amour;* in *A Married Woman* there are passages from Racine's *Bérénice;* and a long extract from Louis Ferdinand Céline's *Voyage au bout de la nuit;* in *Two or Three Things I Know About Her* Vance Packard is quoted. If Godard finds a piece of writing which fits in with the theme or mood of his film, he does not hesitate to use it. 'People in life quote as they please,' he said, 'so we have the right to quote as we please.'[4] He is, however, aware that many of his detractors find this infuriating and at one point in *Two or Three Things I Know About Her* he seems to be poking fun at his jackdaw mind. There is a scene in a café where two characters (named Bouvard and Pecuchet after the pedants created by Gustave Flaubert in his last, unfinished novel) are seen ploughing through hundreds of books, reading out random phrases from each one, and writing them down. As in the game of consequences, the effect is an amusing mixture of freak connections and non-sequiturs.

All Godard's films, even the most serious, contain funny episodes. Many people find this disconcerting but he refuses to accept rules about what should, and should not appear in certain types of film. Nevertheless, in *A Married Woman* and *Two or Three Things I Know About Her,* humour is used to ridicule the ills in society. Social and political satire are not Godard's concern in *A Woman is a Woman,* with its absurd gags, its in-jokes, and its parody of the musical comedy. Certain episodes in the film, do, however, take on greater sociological significance in the light of his later development: the 'documentary' shots of people in the street; the strip-club where women 'prostitute' themselves and are treated as objects; the scene where Angela and Emile refuse to talk to each other but communicate by book-titles; and above all the episode where two police officers enter the flat looking for a suspect. Their manner and the remarks made about the communist newspaper Emile is reading, create threatening undertones, since the film was made during the period of France's Algerian problems. This incident, which prefigures the scene in *Two or Three Things I Know About Her* where the police can be seen hustling off a manacled youth, hints at a repressive society beyond the world of Angela, Emile and Alfred.

Although *A Woman is a Woman* contains the seeds of Godard's later development, it is, undeniably, a lightweight film. The director, himself, described it as a ' sickly child ' but admitted that he was very fond of it. It was, of course, the first film in which Godard used scope, colour and direct sound, but, above all, *A Woman is a Woman* was the first film fully to display the charisma of Anna Karina and has been called a documentary on the Danish actress Godard had just married. He exploited her accented French right down to the final, untranslatable pun. He captured her exuberance and focussed on the wistful beauty of her face. Godard's use of Anna Karina is the most directly personal element in his work; her presence in his films adds an element of romanticism which counteracts his irony and alienation techniques. There is one striking scene where Angela reacts to a photograph of Emile with another woman. For two or three minutes Godard holds her face in close up, apart from the odd cut to the photograph in question. An Aznavour record is playing on the juke box and the words of the song are rather cynical but, as she stares into the camera, hurt and bewildered, her eyes brimming with tears, Godard creates a moment of intense lyricism. ' There is a famous legend ', he wrote in an article of 1952, ' which has it that Griffith, moved by the beauty of his leading lady, invented the close-up in order to capture it in greater detail. Paradoxically, therefore, the simplest close-up is also the most moving '.[5]

Lyricism is conspicuously absent in *A Married Woman* where Godard used a different actress, Macha Méril. Many people felt that he was mistaken but, as Tom Milne pointed out in his introduction to the American edition of the script, ' Karina is almost magically personal: those wide, startled eyes, that grave total absorption would have destroyed the smooth surface texture of *A Married Woman* '. In this film Godard attempts to record human behaviour with clinical detachment. It could be argued that he is working from a false premise since he is not observing the words and actions of real people, but of characters he has, himself, created. His intention is not, however, to achieve documentary-style realism but to use an unemotional approach in order to make the spectator reflect, in the abstract, on certain problems.

Charlotte is involved with two men but, as Godard shows, there is virtually no difference between her marriage to Robert and her affair with Pierre. He stresses the similarities in the conversations she has with both men, and visually underlines these verbal parallels in his presentation of the love scenes. Chronology is ignored and a succession of images appear on the screen. These fragment the naked bodies, breaking them into objects that exist in their own right. The sequences have great formal beauty but they are totally unerotic and they depersonalise the individuals involved.

Throughout *A Married Woman*, Godard discreetly avoids recording any display of emotions in his characters. When Charlotte is in tears, at the end of the film, he does not show her face in close-up (as with Anna Karina in *A Woman is a Woman*) but focuses instead on the lovers' disembodied hands, engaging and disengaging. The effect of this clinical approach is to play down the individuality of the characters in the film and to highlight the situations in which they find themselves. As it was shown by the use of the definite article in the original, censored title of the film — *The Married Woman* — Godard wished to make a general rather than a specific comment on the marital state. When Charlotte says that she is sad at the impossibility of knowing the people she sees in the streets, or when Robert declares that another human being is ' like a house you can't enter ', the director does not wish to arouse sympathy for his characters, and has encouraged the actors to give distant, flat performances. His concern is to direct the attention beyond individuals, to the problem of human relationships in general, to the crucial existentialist dichotomy between subjectivity and objectivity, and to the whole question of communication. How can human beings know each other? When Charlotte questions Pierre (who is an actor) on sincerity, Godard is raising the problem of truth and falsehood. He already touched on this in *A Woman is a Woman* (in the scene where Angela is dismayed to find that the expression on Alfred's face does not change when he tells a lie) but the approach in *A Married Woman* is not only more clinical but more sociological.

The problems of human relationships are shown to be aggravated by modern society. Godard satirises its false values in the scene where Charlotte and Pierre describe their apartment and possessions in the language of a publicity blurb. Throughout the film he cuts to shots of posters and advertisements which dominate modern life, turning the female body into an object, creating false needs, and promising instant happiness on the purchase of certain articles. He is fascinated by the barrage of signs assailing modern man, and uses these, often ironically, to counterpoint the action of the film, sometimes splitting up words to form new ones.

In *A Married Woman* Godard shows that man is a prisoner of the consumer society — hence the references to concentration camps and the snatch of soundtrack from *Night and Fog* — but he does not wish the spectator to be a prisoner of his film. At one point he suddenly switches to negative images; he includes a number of interviews or monologues where the main characters, almost but not quite, step out of the characters they are playing; and he constantly disrupts the narrative line. The end result is a complex film which does not fit into any accepted cinematic genre. It is a collage of disparate elements; it is a frank but abstract sex film; it is a sociological essay which contains clandestine meetings, complicated taxi journeys, and long tracking shots that could well form parts of a Hitchcock thriller.

Two or Three Things I Know About Her also defies conventional classification. Again Godard casts a critical gaze on modern society and punctuates the film with shots of signs and advertisements. Again he distances the spectator, even quoting Brecht when he introduces Marina Vlady, first as herself and then as the character she is playing. Again he briefly dislocates the chronology — when Juliette's mini goes through the car wash and when she and her husband drive into a filling station. But even more so than either *A Woman is a Woman* or *A Married Woman, Two or Three Things I Know About Her* is a film about film, 'cinema and apologia of cinema', as Godard himself said of Renoir's *Paris Does Strange Things*. In his whispered commentary the director reflects on his art, discussing his choices, questioning his means of expression, and explaining his aims.

At the same time the film is a document on contemporary France: the *she* of the title refers not to the housewife, Juliette Janson, but to the whole 'région parisienne' which is undergoing a drastic transformation. Godard suggests the idea of change by shots of construction sites, half-finished motorways, cranes etc., all of which are part of what he calls a 'complex'. 'This complex,' he wrote, 'and its parts (Juliette being the one I have chosen to describe in greater detail, in order to suggest that the other parts also exist in depth) must be described and talked about as both objects and subjects'.[6] This reveals the influence of the poet, Francis Ponge, whose intention is to convey the reality of natural objects and to evoke the sensation of their presence. The long close-up of the burning tip of a cigarette in *Two or Three Things I Know About Her* can be directly compared to Ponge's prose poem, *La cigarette*, in his collection *Le parti pris des choses*.

Godard pays as much attention to cigarettes, books, radios, trees, signs, cars, garages, and buildings, as to people, since both form part of the vast complex he is trying to describe. Whenever possible he attempts to give a 'subjective description of objects' by going inside buildings, by 'settings seen from the inside, where the world is outside'. At the same time people will be seen as objects, as in *A Married Woman*, but periodically they break off a conversation and speak aloud their thoughts, exteriorising their stream of consciousness. What they are thinking is often banal, but it reminds us that, although they are objects in our field of perception, people are conscious beings who exist '*pour soi*', to use Sartrian terms.

Godard's examination of Paris and its suburbs reveals a world where people and things do not live in harmony: people become objects and certain objects become more 'real' than people. The American war-correspondent uses Juliette and her friend as objects, photographing them as they parade naked around the room, dehumanizing them even more by insisting that they cover their heads with bags. The soulless new housing complexes, springing up around Paris, are built without any real consideration for their future inhabitants. As was shown by the article in a French weekly, on which the film was based, many housewives on these estates resort to prostitution to help to pay the bills and to fulfil the needs created by the consumer society. Prostitution is a recurrent theme in Godard's work; in *Two or Three Things I Know About Her* he implies that everybody is forced to prostitute himself in modern society. He places the blame for this on the Gaullist government of the time, but also sees the complex he is examining in an international perspective. There are numerous references to Vietnam, suggesting perhaps that the war there is merely an extreme example of the repression which can be seen in the everyday life of Western capitalism. Godard does not, however, feel that a workers' revolution is possible, and he certainly does not consider Soviet communism to be an answer, as is made apparent in the scene with the fictitious Russian Nobel prizewinner. His attitude to official communism was not to change when he committed himself to working for a socialist revolution after 1968.

Two or Three Things I Know About Her documents the ills of capitalism but the mood of the film is reflective rather than polemical. This is evident in the meditation which accompanies the sustained close-up of a cup of black coffee. As bubbles from the sugar rise to the surface, Godard's voice can be heard reflecting on society, on existential questions, on language and the impossibility of conveying through words (which define and limit) the complexity of the world. There is a note of calm pessimism in this, which is echoed in the conversation at the end of the film, where death appears as the final absurdity of life.

Although humour is present in both *Two or Three Things I Know About Her* and *A Married Woman*, Godard has come a long way from the frivolity of *A Woman is a Woman*. In his increasing attempts to deal with themes and problems, usually left to other disciplines, he has created new means of expression, and expanded traditional notions of cinema. At the same time he has brilliantly captured the atmosphere of modern Paris and revealed the underlying mood of French society in the sixties.

[1] *The Films of Jean-Luc Godard* (Studio Vista) p. 135
[2] *Godard on Godard* (Secker & Warburg) p. 173
[3] *Godard on Godard* (Secker & Warburg) p. 173
[4] *Godard on Godard* (Secker & Warburg) p. 173
[5] *Godard on Godard* (Secker & Warburg) p. 28
[6] *Godard on Godard* (Secker & Warburg) p. 239

A WOMAN IS A WOMAN

CREDITS:

Production Company	Rome-Paris Films (Paris)
Producers	Georges de Beauregard
	Carlo Ponti
Production Manager	Philippe Dussart
Director	Jean-Luc Godard
Assistant Director	Francis Cognany
Script	Jean-Luc Godard
Director of Photography	Raoul Coutard
Editors	Agnès Guillemot
	Lila Herman
Art Director	Bernard Evein
Music	Michel Legrand
Song ' Angela's Song '	Michel Legrand
	Jean-Luc Godard
Sound	Guy Villette

CAST:

Angela	Anna Karina
Alfred Lubitsch	Jean-Paul Belmondo
Emile Récamier	Jean-Claude Brialy
Suzanne	Marie Dubois
First Girl	Nicole Paquin
Second Girl	Marion Sarraut

18

A WOMAN IS A WOMAN

Brief credits appear over close-ups of main characters.

VOICE off: *LIGHTS! CAMERA! ACTION!*

A song is heard in the background as ANGELA walks through a crowded Paris street. She wears a light raincoat and holds an opened, red umbrella in her hand. She comes through a café door, smiling.

ANGELA to BARMAID: *A white coffee . . . very white!*

She leans with her back to the bar and takes off her gloves.

EMILE, wearing coat, hat and scarf, approaches the bar.

EMILE to BARMAID: *A white coffee . . . green!*

ANGELA looks at him, moves to the juke-box and selects a record.

ANGELA comes back to the bar and watches EMILE drink his coffee.

ANGELA to BARMAID: *What's the time?*

BARMAID: *Five-thirty!*

ANGELA drinking hurriedly: *It's too hot, I haven't got time!*

She turns towards camera and winks.

Outside the café, she crosses the busy street and goes into a bookshop.

ANGELA to BOOKSELLER: *Hello! How're things?*

BOOKSELLER: *Hi! Okay.*

ANGELA sees EMILE in another part of the bookshop, selecting a book. He opens one entitled ' I Am Expecting a Baby '. He waves it at ANGELA.

ANGELA leafs through a magazine. (*Still*) She lifts it to cover her face, then lowers it a little and gives EMILE a broad grin.

EMILE shows a book to a small child.

EMILE: *How about this?*

The MOTHER quickly hustles her child out of the bookshop.

MOTHER: *Come along!*

EMILE approaches ANGELA.

EMILE: *Hello!*

ANGELA: *Are you still angry?*

19

EMILE: *No, my angel.*

ANGELA moving off: *Do you love me then?*

EMILE: *Yes . . . my angel.*

> ANGELA picks up a postcard showing two little ducks. She shows it to EMILE.

ANGELA: *Oh, look how pretty this postcard is, Emile!*

EMILE off: *Why are you crying?*

ANGELA: *Because . . . I should like to be both little yellow animals at the same time.*

EMILE: *You always want impossible things!*

> ANGELA shrugs her shoulders.

ANGELA: *Well, I've got to go.*

> She blows him a kiss and walks off.

> EMILE also blows her a kiss, hitting a woman passing by. He bows to the woman and lifts his hat.

> ANGELA now walks along the crowded street.

NEWSBOY off: *Extra! Extra! France-Soir, Paris, Presse, Le Monde. Get your Figaro Littéraire . . . get your Marie-Claire. . . .*

> ANGELA runs into ALFRED.

ALFRED: *Hi, Angela!*

ANGELA: *Hello.*

ALFRED: *You look sad.*

ANGELA: *Me? Not in the least!*

ALFRED: *I've got to talk to you.*

ANGELA: *Why don't you run up to the Trocadero and see if I'm in?*

ALFRED: *Really, Angela, it's serious.*

ANGELA: *Haven't got time. I'm late.*

ALFRED: *What're you thinking about?*

ANGELA: *Nothing!* Pause. *I'm thinking that I exist.*

> She walks away.

ALFRED to camera: *Exit Angela!*

> ANGELA hurries through the main door of a strip-tease club.

ANGELA to a passing GIRL: *All right?*

GIRL: *Okay!*

> ANGELA walks past the bar, a strip-tease act is in progress on the floor. There are a few men sitting at the tables which are covered with checkered tablecloths.
>
> A blonde, dressed in red and carrying a hatbox and an umbrella, is doing her act.

ANGELA off stage, talks to another GIRL and pets a white rabbit on a table.

ANGELA: *Hello . . . hello, bunny!*

GIRL: *Did you pick up my France-Soir for the horoscopes?*

ANGELA gives her the newspaper.

ANGELA: *Yes, yes . . . here it is. Will you look up mine? I'm Virgo.* She walks off.

SECOND GIRL: *Angela, you're on before Danièle, get a move on!* Another shot of the blonde doing her act.

ANGELA off: *How come I'm on first?*

SECOND GIRL: *Oh, I don't know, ask Luciano!*

Cut to the floor show. A man now unzips the red dress of the performer. The blonde begins to take off her dress.

ANGELA walks on, taking off her raincoat.

She stops at the bar.

ANGELA to BARMAN: *A packet of Gitanes.*

BARMAN: *That's 10,500 francs you owe me.*

ANGELA stretching out her hand for the cigarettes: *Don't fuss, I'll pay.*

She sits down at a table, next to a GIRL sipping a drink through a straw.

ANGELA to GIRL: *Has Dominique got back from the hospital?*

GIRL: *Yes, yes . . . She'll bring you your little gadget.*

ANGELA fingering a locket around the GIRL's neck: *Hey, what's that? Oh, it's really cute.*

GIRL: *I bought it at the Galeries Lafayette.*

ANGELA: *It's really sweet!*

Cut to the floor show. The blonde is half naked, walking off in a pair of striped panties. A man walks after her, picking up the red dress, hatbox and umbrella.

Cut to ANGELA, talking to a GIRL.

ANGELA: *Have you looked in France-Soir yet?*

GIRL: *Here we are . . . Virgo . . . A happy event soon!*

ANGELA snatching away the newspaper and smiling: *No kidding!*

GIRL: *That's great! . . . Have you seen my new number?*

ANGELA: *No.*

GIRL: *Look!*

She quickly walks behind a pillar, wearing her ordinary clothing and reappears immediately, dressed in coloured feathers

21

from head to toe.

ANGELA: *Oh, it's fantastic.*

MAN approaching: *Hey, Angela, did you go to the Champs Elysées?*

ANGELA running up the stairs: *No, I did not!*

MAN: *Why not?*

ANGELA: *Because!*

MAN: *What's that supposed to mean?*

ANGELA turning her head: *It means that there are more important things than going to the Champs Elysées.*

MAN: *Hurry, Angela, you're on.*

DOMINIQUE off: *Angela!*

> ANGELA appears from behind a red curtain.
>
> She is undressing.

ANGELA: *Yes, I'm here!*

DOMINIQUE: *I got your little gadget for you.*

MAN off: *Dominique, get a move on!*

ANGELA: *Will you explain it to me?*

DOMINIQUE throwing a package into the air and catching it: *Yes, it's easy . . . I'll put it in the drawer.*

ANGELA: *Okay!*

> In the dressing room, ANGELA smokes a cigarette, unfolds a piece of paper, and reads it as she kicks off her shoes.

MAN'S VOICE off: *You will become like the man who has seen the man . . . who has seen the man, who has seen the man, who has seen the bear.*

> ANGELA sits in front of her mirror and puts on a sailor's cap. She walks through a corridor, dressed in a white sailor-suit, and leans towards a GIRL reading.

GIRL reading slowly: *The creations of art are the forty days of nature's glorious life . . .*

> ANGELA shrugs her shoulders, laughs and walks on.

ANGELA to another GIRL passing: *Hi!*

GIRL: *Hi!*

> ANGELA is now setting a tape recorder. A tune starts playing; she beats time with her finger, steps on the stage from behind a curtain, and smiles at the audience. (*Still*)
>
> During ANGELA's song and strip-tease act, only close-ups of her face are shown. The lights change from white to blue to red. Intermittently, the camera cuts to different men watching

her act. One sips his drink and smacks his lips, another looks at her through opera glasses, a third just smokes and writes something in a diary.

ANGELA singing:

> Everybody wonders why
> Men all stare when I pass by.
> But it isn't hard to see
> Why the boys all go for me.
> I have pretty breasts
> And my eyes are bright,
> I've a sailor's collar
> And pants that fit just right.
> I just really hate
> Rising before noon,
> But just stroke my back,
> And I'll be sure to swoon.
> I always agree
> When a boy says ' Come with me '.
> Saying no simply annoys
> The boys.
> I can be a bad girl,
> I can be a pest,
> But the men never complain
> 'Cos I look nice undressed.

Backstage, ANGELA stands wrapped only in a towel.

ANGELA: *Well, I am going to try it too.*

GIRL: *Go on, do!*

ANGELA walks behind the pillar and quickly reappears, fully dressed in her sweater and skirt.

GIRL: *Fantastic!*

DOMINIQUE approaching: *Well, here it is!*

ANGELA smiling: *How does it work?*

SECOND GIRL passing by: *Well, personally, I prefer the rhythm method!*

DOMINIQUE: *You're joking!*

ANGELA: *Do you really?*

SECOND GIRL: *Really! That's how Chérie got her kid.*

DOMINIQUE: *Don't listen to her. This thing's really scientific.*

MAN approaching: *Bianchini wants some girls for Marseilles, 40,000 francs a week, flat!*
DOMINIQUE: *Oh,* him!

BIANCHINI sits at a table with a couple of girls.
BIANCHINI: *Do you want to sign up?*
FIRST GIRL: *Can I take my travelling iron?*
SECOND GIRL: *Hum . . . Hum . . .*
FIRST GIRL: *Where would we live?*
BIANCHINI: *In a hotel.*
SECOND GIRL: *Would we have a place to wash our clothes?*
BIANCHINI: *Of course.* He sees ANGELA approaching the table. *Are you coming, too, Angela?*
ANGELA: *No. I'm not interested. Anyway, I hate the Côte d'Azure.*
ANGELA leaves, adjusting one stocking then another.
BIANCHINI watching her: *Red stockings, blue stockings . . .*
ANGELA flings open another curtain on her way out.
ANGELA to more GIRLS: *I'm off! Ciao.*
She walks past another stripper on the floor, and then by the bar.

Cut to ANGELA and ALFRED in the street. Individual close-ups.
ALFRED: *You, Angela, no time!*
ANGELA: *Me, Angela, no time!*
Cut to a busy square. ALFRED puts a note under the wipers of a parked car.
A MAN, wearing a cap and raincoat, approaches him.
MAN to ALFRED: *52,000 francs.*
ALFRED hands in pockets: *Me?*
MAN: *Yes, you! Don't you owe 52,000 francs to the Hotel Bikini?*
ALFRED: *Me?*
MAN: *Didn't you leave on 9th of July without paying your bill?*
ALFRED reaches into his pocket and produces a diary.
ALFRED: *Hold on, I can tell you. . . . I write everything I do in my diary. October, September, July. . . .* He leafs through the pages. . . . *Hold on. . . . July 20th . . . here we are. . . . July 19th. . . . You see, you're quite wrong. Look!* He points. *10 a.m., telephone Popol for a loan. Noon, lunch in the snack bar on the Rue de Strasbourg.*
NEWSBOY off: *Extra! France-Soir, Paris-Presse, Le Monde . . .*
ALFRED: *. . . 5.30 . . . why . . . you're quite right.*

24

NEWSBOY off: *Get your Figaro Littéraire!*

ALFRED: *. . . Left the Hotel Bikini without paying the bill.*

NEWSBOY off: *Get your Marie-Claire!*

MAN: *Well, are you going to pay me?*

ALFRED walking off: *No, never.*

MAN shouting after him: *Stupid creep!*

> The camera cuts from ALFRED to the MAN, as they each walk off in different directions, crossing the street and shouting at each other.

ALFRED: *Cretin!*

MAN: *Dirty bastard!*

ALFRED: *Stinking queer!*

MAN: *Dirty bugger!*

ALFRED: *Bloody Jew!*

MAN: *Fascist!*

ALFRED: *Sodomite!*

> ANGELA is walking in the crowded street.

> ALFRED runs up to her.

ALFRED walking beside her: *Why didn't you wait for me?*

ANGELA: *Because I've got more important things to do.*

ALFRED: *Don't you think it's important that I want you?*

ANGELA: *Isn't it funny? It's not nearly as sunny as it was an hour ago.*

ALFRED: *Nothing funny about that.*

ANGELA: *No? . . . All right, then. There's nothing funny about it!*

ALFRED: *Then why did you say it was funny in the first place?*

ANGELA: *I don't know! I'm sad.*

ALFRED: *You're a funny girl.*

ANGELA: *What's happened to Agnes? Has she had her baby?*

ALFRED: *I dunno . . . not my business any more.*

ANGELA: *You're a funny boy!*

ALFRED: *You really don't care if I want you or not?*

ANGELA: *If you put the adjective in front of the word instead of after, in French . . . does it still have the same meaning?*

ALFRED: *What do you mean?*

ANGELA: *For instance, is a happy event different from an event that's happy?*

ALFRED: *Is that what you're sad about?*

ANGELA: *No.*

She runs on ahead.

ALFRED shouting after her: *Then why?*

ANGELA: *Because I should like to be in a musical . . .*

Cut to ANGELA suddenly wearing a blue dress, trimmed with white fur. She is dancing to rising music, Gene Kelly style. Behind her is an old building with a staircase to her flat. There are some old dustbins outside; a couple are kissing in a doorway.

ANGELA off: *. . . with Cyd Charisse . . . and Gene Kelly . . . choreo-graphy . . . by Bob Fosse . . .*

ALFRED runs up to ANGELA, still by the staircase but dressed once more in her raincoat.

ALFRED: *Angela.*

ANGELA: *Now what?*

ALFRED: *You forgot to say good-bye to me.*

He pats her behind; she kicks out at him, running up the stairs.

ALFRED: *Missed!*

ALFRED leans against the wall. ANGELA pauses.

ANGELA playing with her beret: *Yesterday, you asked me why I love Emile and not you . . . Because he's handsome and clever and you're not.*

ALFRED: *I'm very clever.*

ANGELA: *Really?* She walks up one step and pauses. *I bet you can't do everything I do!*

ALFRED: *Bet I can!*

Loud music. ALFRED is imitating ANGELA's every pose. First they stand with arms outstretched, then they crouch with back of hand under the chin; then on one leg with arms in the air. (*Still*) Finally they crouch back to back. She turns, gives him a kick and runs up the stairs. He follows her, turns back and shouts something at her.

Inside ANGELA's flat. She comes through the door, takes off her coat and runs into the kitchen. She opens the oven door, looks inside and closes it. She goes back through the hall and knocks on the door next to hers. It opens and a NEIGHBOUR appears.

ANGELA: *Thanks for the roast-beef.*

NEIGHBOUR: *No trouble, Madame Récamier!*

26

ANGELA returns, lights the oven and goes to the living room. She looks at herself in the mirror and plays with her hair.

She goes into the bedroom, makes the bed by lifting the blanket and throwing herself on top of the bed.

SUZANNE stands in the street, looking up at ANGELA's balcony.

SUZANNE shouting: *Angela . . . Angela, I've got something to tell you!*

ANGELA appears on the balcony.

ANGELA shouting down: *Not now!*

ANGELA is back in her flat. She draws the curtains, dances away from the window to the mirror. She sings to herself as she dances, watching every movement.

Finally she sits down on a chair, picks up her little package, opens it and reads aloud.

ANGELA: *Madame, the CD Indicator enables you to know . . . with scientific exactitude . . . the days when conception is possible . . . with scientific precision. Take the black cylinder in your right hand . . . until the triangle is opposite the nought. There . . . it's at zero. . . . The days on which you can conceive a child . . . will now appear in the window of the black cylinder. November 10th . . . What's the date today?*

She rushes into the kitchen to look at a wall calendar. It says — 10th November.

She hears someone at the door and smiles.

EMILE, wearing a hat and scarf, comes through the door.

EMILE: *Hi!*

ANGELA: *Hey! Where did you get that scarf?*

EMILE: *I bought myself an early Christmas present.* He hangs up the scarf. *And here . . . I got you a Marie-Claire.*

He goes into another room, throwing the magazine towards her.

ANGELA looks pensive, still holding her gadget.

EMILE off: *Is the match over?*

ANGELA: *What match?*

She puts on an apron. EMILE comes into the kitchen.

EMILE: *Hell! . . . Angela. . . . Royal vs. Barcelona. . . .* He turns and leaves the kitchen. *I told you to turn the radio on . . . always have to do everything myself!*

ANGELA: *Bah!*

EMILE comes back into the kitchen and touches her back.

27

EMILE: *What's the matter now? . . . What is it?*

ANGELA: *First of all, before acting out our little farce, we should bow to the audience.*

Through the opened door, which frames them both, they bow and smile at the camera.

EMILE: *Okay . . . what have I done?*

ANGELA: *You don't love me!*

EMILE: *Listen to that little idiot! Listen to her! I love only you . . .*

ANGELA turns and walks from room to room.

EMILE follows her.

EMILE: *What's wrong with you? What's wrong? I love only you . . . your eyes, your neck, your shoulder . . . your waist.*

They stop at the front door.

ANGELA: *Okay, okay.*

She points to his feet.

EMILE: *. . . your feet.*

ANGELA goes off to the kitchen. EMILE follows her, pats her behind and runs away.

ANGELA follows him with a broom in her hand.

ANGELA: *Emile, instead of making a fool of yourself, why don't you sweep the floor?*

EMILE takes the broom from her, pretends to play it as though it were a guitar. (*Still*)

EMILE singing: *I love only you. . . . I love only you. . . . I love only . . .*

He goes to the radio and turns it on. Now he makes sweeping movements in rhythm to the commentator's words.

RADIO off: *The ball to Di Stéfano, Di Stéfano has the ball. . . . Oh! . . . he's racing down the right wing . . . exactly the way Stanley Matthews used to. . . . It's fantastic!*

EMILE, still gesturing with the broom, pretends to sweep. He finally goes into the hall and throws the broom into the kitchen.

RADIO off: *It's Shakespearian. . . .Alfrédo the Great . . . the Julius Caesar of the football field . . . now the centre passes to Del Sol, Del Sol to Puskas . . . Puskas to Del Sol . . . Del Sol to Di Stéfano . . . Di Stéfano to Del Sol. . . . I'm overcome by the greatness of the Royal team today. . . . Del Sol charges into the Barcelona penalty area . . . oooh! . . . Quite extraordinary! . . . Del Sol is standing alone in front of Ramallets. . . . Careful . . . he shoots . . . oooh!*

The broom hits ANGELA's back, as she is wiping her hands on a kitchen towel. She picks up the broom and puts it away.

ANGELA: *I haven't finished yet.*

EMILE off: *Are we eating soon?*

ANGELA opening the oven door: *It's over-cooked!*

She pauses, looking perplexed, and starts towards the living room.

EMILE is seated at the table, which is set ready for a meal. He is reading a newspaper.

RADIO off: *Del Sol to Puskas, Puskas to Del Sol . . . Del Sol to Di Stéfano . . .*

ANGELA turns off the radio and stands by the table, looking at EMILE.

ANGELA: *Would you rather have fish or meat for dinner tonight?* No reply. *Emile!*

EMILE absorbed in the paper: *Fish.*

ANGELA: *Well, if you had wanted meat, what kind of meat would you have preferred?*

EMILE: *I don't know. . . . Veal.*

ANGELA: *And if you wanted beef instead of veal, would you have chosen roast-beef or steak?*

EMILE: *Steak, definitely!*

ANGELA: *Well, if you had said roast-beef, would you have wanted it well done or very rare?*

EMILE: *Very rare.*

ANGELA sitting down at the table (*Still*): *Well, my love, it's not your night because my roast-beef is a little overcooked.* Pause. *Are you angry?*

EMILE from behind his newspaper: *No. We're not going to quarrel over a thing like that.*

ANGELA pouring some wine: *That's a pity, it might have settled my nerves.*

EMILE abstractedly: *Oh, I went to see Gérardine. He says it's okay for Sunday.*

He turns his newspaper to another page.

ANGELA: *Oh, really?*

EMILE: *At first he didn't want to, but he came round in the end.*

ANGELA smiling and leaning forward: *Marvellous!*

EMILE: *Yes, in Prince's Park, at the beginning of the meeting . . .*

ANGELA playing with her hair: *Oh, yes? . . . Would you rather I made boiled eggs instead?*

EMILE: *Of course, my love.*

ANGELA: *All right, but on one condition.*

EMILE looking up: *What?*

ANGELA: *I want a baby.*

EMILE: *A baby?*

ANGELA rubbing her nose and looking anxious: *Yes.*

EMILE putting his paper away: *Yes, all right Angela, it's a deal.*

ANGELA smiling: *You're not kidding? You don't mind?*

EMILE: *No, of course not, I'm not heartless. . . . We'll have a child as soon as we're married.*

ANGELA jumping up excitedly: *Then let's get married . . . but I haven't got my birth certificate. . . . I'll write to Copenhagen straight away.*

She joyfully dances away towards the mirror. (*Still*)

EMILE gets up and moves towards his bicycle, which leans against the wall of the living room.

EMILE: *Oh, there's no hurry!*

ANGELA: *But I don't understand . . .*

She moves towards him, hands in pockets of her apron.

EMILE examining a bicycle part: *Yes, Angela . . . if we had a child, we'd get married right away. . . . But that's not the case.*

ANGELA pauses, then turns away dejectedly.

ANGELA: *Well, I want a baby!*

EMILE: *All right then, we'll see.* There is a pause as he plays with his bicycle. *And what did the fellow at the Lido have to say?*

ANGELA: *I didn't go.*

She sits down at the table and plays with her hair. EMILE starts riding his bicycle round and round the table. (*Still*)

EMILE: *You must be crazy, Angela. The Lido's important, a hell of a lot more important than the Zodiac.*

ANGELA: *Why are you so cruel?*

She picks at a piece of bread.

EMILE: *What've I done? What've I done now?*

He continues to ride his bicycle round the table, looking very serious.

ANGELA: *Exactly!*

EMILE: *Exactly, what?*

ANGELA: *Can't you talk to me in a nicer voice?*

EMILE: *What kind of a voice?*

ANGELA: *A . . . a deeper voice. . . . You make my ears ache!*

EMILE gets off the bicycle and replaces it against the wall.

EMILE indignantly: *I have a very nice, very deep voice!*

ANGELA: *You certainly don't!*

EMILE: *I don't have a deep voice?*

ANGELA mimicking him: *I don't have a deep voice?*

EMILE: *You* can't *talk! You can't even pronounce your R's.*

He sits down at the table, facing ANGELA.

ANGELA: *Me? Of course I can. . . . R . . . R . . . R . . . R . . . R . . . R . . .*
She produces a continuous R sound in time to background
music.

EMILE: *Pathetic! . . . R . . . R . . . R . . . R . . . R . . . R . . . R . . .*
He sings out the R, a tone higher.

ANGELA warbles even higher, gesticulating with her arms.

EMILE tries again, this time for much longer.

ANGELA takes over, determined not to be outdone.

Pause.

ANGELA: *Why do women always have to suffer?*

EMILE: *Because women are the cause of all suffering . . . or* woman
is the cause of all suffering! You can say it either way in French!

ANGELA licking her fingers: *Shut your face or I'll hit you so hard
you won't have a face left to shut!* Pause. *Do you want me to?*

EMILE changing the subject: *Did you take the morning paper?*

ANGELA goes into the kitchen and opens the newspaper. She
throws it at EMILE through the door.

ANGELA: *I despise you . . . here, you dirty communist!*

EMILE off: *Oh, come on, Angela, that's enough!*

ANGELA picks up an egg and immediately drops it on the floor.
(*Still*)
She bends down and covers her face.

EMILE off: *Here we go!*

ANGELA: *I don't know anymore if I should laugh or cry!*

EMILE comes into the kitchen and lights a cigarette.

EMILE: *Well, I think that women who cry are very ugly.*

ANGELA: *No. . . . I think it's just the opposite . . . that's what
Agnes was saying. . . . There's nothing as beautiful as a woman in
tears.* Pause. *Women who don't cry should be boycotted!*

31

EMILE in close-up, the cigarette in his mouth.

ANGELA off: *I think modern women are stupid, trying to limitate . . . no, that isn't right, is it?*

ANGELA in close-up, tears pouring down her face.

ANGELA: *No. . . . I think women who don't cry are stupid. . . . Modern women just want to imitate men! . . . Anyway, I'm fed up with all of you! You can look after yourself!*

She runs into the hall and buries her face in EMILE's scarf.

EMILE off: ' *All of you* '?

ANGELA turning her face to him: *You can do your own cooking!*

She moves towards the bedroom, EMILE bars the door.

EMILE: ' *All of you* '? . . . *Just what do you mean by that?*

ANGELA: *You needn't think you're the only man in town!*

She walks past him, magazine in hand.

EMILE following her: *Meaning what, exactly?*

ANGELA: *I want a baby!*

They both move to sit on the bed.

EMILE: *There's plenty of time. Come on, be reasonable . . . really . . . what have I said now?*

ANGELA: *I want a baby in the next twenty-four hours.*

EMILE playing with her hair: *You're incredible, Angela! Listen, you know about Anquetil in the Tour de France . . . every time his wife came to see him, he'd drop another place behind . . . and I have to be on form for Sunday.*

ANGELA: *Well, if* that's *how you feel, I'm going out!*

She gets off the bed and goes towards the door.

EMILE stands up too, and begins to imitate all her words and gestures. He follows her around the flat.

EMILE: *Well, if that's how you feel, I'm going out!*

ANGELA: *Exactly!*

EMILE: *Exactly!*

ANGELA: *You think I'm mad, but I'm perfectly sane!*

EMILE: *You think I'm mad, but I'm perfectly sane!*

ANGELA: *I'm getting a plane to Copenhagen.*

EMILE: *I'm getting a plane to Copenhagen.*

EMILE: *Fine. You do what you want!*

EMILE: *Fine. You do what you want!*

They both finally end up sitting on the bed as before.

ANGELA: *I want a child!*

EMILE: *I don't see why, all of a sudden.*

ANGELA: *Because I'm asking you. Because I thought you loved me . . . but since you don't. . . .* She gets up . . . *it's quite simple, I shall just ask anyone, the first man I see.*

She gets up again, moving towards the hall.

EMILE following her: *Bet you don't!*

ANGELA: *Bet I do!*

EMILE: *All right! Go ahead. Go on, it'll do you good!*

There is a loud knock on the door.

He pushes her playfully towards it.

ANGELA opens the door to two MEN in raincoats.

FIRST MAN showing his identity card: *Madame! Police! A terrorist has just thrown a bomb on the Boulevard . . . mind if we look around?*

ANGELA turning: *Emile!*

The two MEN walk through the door and past EMILE who is leaning against the wall. EMILE nods to them; they start looking around the living room. They look through the balcony windows, draw back the curtains. They walk past the table; one of them picks up a piece of cheese and stops to smell it. They walk back through the kitchen and stop to look at EMILE reading the paper. One of them takes the paper from EMILE and looks at the headline.

FIRST MAN: *I see you read l'Humanité . . . keep up the good work!*

They leave through the front door.

ANGELA: *Goodbye, Messieurs.*

EMILE off: *See, I knew you wouldn't dare to ask just anyone! So, how about making me those boiled eggs?*

ANGELA: *Okay. Will you give me a baby?*

EMILE: *Ahh! Just anybody? Okay, I'm going to call Alfred.*

ANGELA horrified: *Alfred? . . . Alfred?*

EMILE looks out through the windows. He turns.

EMILE: *Shall I go ahead?*

ANGELA: *You disgust me! You're a coward!*

EMILE: *All right. I'll do it . . .*

TITLE in large letters on a black background:

EMILE TAKES ANGELA AT HER WORD BECAUSE HE LOVES HER.

ANGELA LETS HERSELF BE CAUGHT IN THE TRAP BECAUSE SHE LOVES HIM.

EMILE picks up the telephone.

EMILE to ANGELA: *You asked for it.* Into telephone. *Alfred, are you there? Come on up!*

ALFRED off: *Why?*

EMILE into telephone: *Come on, hurry up.*

Cut to ANGELA.

ANGELA: *Well, what did you say to him? That I wanted a baby?*

EMILE: *Poor idiot! . . . I said to him: ' Come on up . . .'*

ANGELA: *Did you get the light-bulbs?*

EMILE: *Damn! I forgot.*

ANGELA: *Poor idiot:*

EMILE: *There are limits, you know.*

ANGELA: *I wonder what* that's *supposed to mean?*

EMILE: *Nothing special. It means what it means.*

ANGELA: *You always evade the question . . . what limits?*

EMILE: *I do exactly what you do.*

ANGELA: *Women have the right to evade questions, Monsieur Emile . . . men don't!*

EMILE: *How come?*

ANGELA: *Because!*

She turns and goes up to him after a pause.

ANGELA: *Say something nice to me.*

EMILE: *Just leave me alone, do you mind?*

ANGELA: *Say, please.*

EMILE: *You say, please.*

TITLE in large letters on a black background:

BECAUSE THEY LOVE ONE ANOTHER, EVERYTHING WILL GO WRONG FOR EMILE AND ANGELA. THEY HAVE MADE THE MISTAKE OF THINKING THEY CAN GO TOO FAR. BECAUSE THEIR LOVE IS BOTH MUTUAL AND ETERNAL.

Cut to ALFRED at the front door. EMILE and ANGELA are standing in the hall.

ALFRED: *Hi, Angela!*

ANGELA: *Good-evening.*

ALFRED: *What's up?*

ANGELA: *Emile has something to say to you.*

EMILE: *It's not me. It's Angela.*

ANGELA: *No, it's not. It's Emile.*

EMILE: *Absolutely not!*

ANGELA: *Absolutely not?*

ALFRED: *Well, what is it?*

ANGELA: *It's Emile.*

ALFRED: *Make up your minds! They've got 'A Bout de Souffle' playing on the telly at Marcel's. I don't want to miss it!*

They are all still standing in the hall.

EMILE: *Well, Angela?*

ANGELA: *Well, Emile?*

ALFRED: *Well, Angela-Emile?*

Close-up of EMILE, as he looks embarrassed. He loosens his collar.

EMILE: *Okay, here goes! Do you agree to give this young lady a baby?*

ALFRED looking from EMILE to ANGELA: *What is this . . . a tragedy or a comedy?*

EMILE: *You can't ever be certain with women!*

ANGELA finally making up her mind: *Will you come into the bathroom with me, Alfred?*

ALFRED puzzled to EMILE: *Should I?*

EMILE: *Yes.*

ANGELA pulling ALFRED towards the bathroom: *Are you coming?*

ALFRED turning back towards EMILE: *If it upsets you, just say so!*

EMILE: *Not at all. I'm delighted!*

ANGELA and ALFRED disappear into the bathroom, closing the door.

EMILE, pretending to be very nonchalant, walks towards his bicycle and leans over it.

There is a loud screeching from the bathroom.

EMILE looks up, frowning.

There is a sound of running water from the bathroom.

EMILE looks puzzled.

Inside the bathroom, ANGELA and ALFRED are looking at each other in close-up.

ALFRED: *Why are you doing this?*

ANGELA: *I don't know.*
ALFRED: *Do you want me to stay?*
ANGELA: *Yes.*
ALFRED: *Do you want me to go?*
ANGELA: *Yes.*
ALFRED: *You say ' yes ' to everything. It's stupid!*
ANGELA: *Yes!*

They sit down on the edge of the bath.

EMILE is cycling round the flat.

Suddenly the bathroom door opens and ANGELA comes out, singing to herself. She looks into the mirror, walks past EMILE cycling, picks something off the bookshelf and returns to the bathroom, closing the door.

There is the sound of laughter from the bathroom. EMILE gets off the bicycle, puts it against the wall and walks to the bathroom door. He pauses, goes towards the bookshelf, picks out a book and sits down outside the bathroom door, pretending to read.

Inside the bathroom, ALFRED reads.

ALFRED: *One day, Jesus said to Mathew, ' Get out of the train and pump up my tyres ... '*

EMILE is listening outside the bathroom door.

EMILE shouting: *Can't you see she's just trying it on? . . . Anyway, I'm going down to eat at Marcel's.*

Close-up of ALFRED and ANGELA in the bathroom.

ALFRED: *Me too! 'Bye, Angela.*
ANGELA: *Wait for me!*

ALFRED comes out of the bathroom.

EMILE to ANGELA still in the bathroom: *No. You're a drag.*

EMILE and ALFRED whisper to each other and laugh, looking at the bathroom door. They hide in the hall.

Back in the bathroom, ANGELA looks sadly into the mirror. She straightens her hair.

ANGELA shouting: *Get lost, you stupid bastards!*

She comes out of the bathroom to find EMILE and ALFRED laughing in the hall.

ANGELA: *Haven't you gone yet?*
EMILE: *Who are you coming with, him or me?*
ALFRED: *Yes ... men are just as strange as women.*

36

ANGELA regaining her composure: *With the one who can do the most extraordinary trick.*

She turns to them and smiles winningly.

EMILE stands by the mirror, a dead-pan look on his face. He holds one foot with his hand and turns round and round.

ALFRED pretends to be boxing with a standard lamp.

EMILE folds his hands above his head and imitates a hen. He puts one hand in his pocket and produces an egg. (*Still*)

ALFRED knocks the standard lamp right over.

ANGELA looks at them.

ANGELA: *It's just vulgar entertainment. You're horrid . . . you shouldn't make fun of love.*

ALFRED off: *Let's go! And death to all womankind!*

EMILE off: *Let's get the hell out of here.*

EMILE and ALFRED walk out.

ANGELA rushes to the door, closes it with a kick but it swings open. She kicks it again and it slams shut. She presses her face against it.

ANGELA softly at the door: *I love you. . . . I love you. . . . I love you.*

EMILE off: *What did you say, Angela?*

His face appears at the little grated window.

ANGELA shouting: *I don't love you!*

Sound of laughter from behind the door.

EMILE off: *Okay, Angela, that's just fine!*

ANGELA turns away from the door and walks into the bedroom. She throws herself on the bed, swinging her legs over her head.

She picks up a pillow, goes to the mirror, and slips it under her jumper.

She struts up and down, pretending to be pregnant. She goes to the balcony door and looks out into the night. She removes the pillow from under her jumper and opens another window.

ANGELA into the night: *Farewell, Camille, return to your convent.*

She picks up a book, sits down and begins to read.

ANGELA: *All men are liars, faithless, false . . . garrulous, hypocrites and proud.* She begins to walk around. *One is often deceived in love, often hurt, often unhappy. And when you reach the edge of the grave, you turn round to look back on your life and say ' I have suffered, I have sometimes been deceived, but I have loved.* She puts on her raincoat. *It is I who have lived and no substitute being created by my pride and my distress . . .*

Bright neon signs on a black background.

Inside the café, ALFRED and EMILE are sitting at a table with DOMINIQUE and MARION.

EMILE sips his drink and looks out of the window. He gets up and goes off.

EMILE off: *I'll be back.*

DOMINIQUE: *Why do men who are going away always say ' I'll be back '?*

MARION: *Because they're all cowards!*

ALFRED: *It makes up for the fact that all women are dishonest.*

He looks out of the window.

A street scene at night. EMILE and ANGELA are standing outside a radio and television shop.

A television set is on, and the camera cuts from the couple to the television screen.

ANGELA: *If that's how it is, I shall sulk.*

EMILE: *Here we go! She's sulking.*

ANGELA: *I hope you've noticed that I'm sulking.*

EMILE: *No. I'm taking great care not to notice.*

ANGELA: *You must. Otherwise there's no point in sulking.*

EMILE: *No. If I don't sulk then you'll stop wanting to.*

ANGELA: *Men always have to have the last word.*

EMILE: *Women always need to see themselves as victims.*

ANGELA: *Oh, very well, I shan't sulk any more.*

EMILE: *In that case, it's my turn to sulk!*

Cut to the café.

ALFRED to the girls: *What shall we do?*

MARION: *Whatever you like!*

EMILE returns to the table and sits down.

EMILE: *We'll go with you down to the Zodiac.*

MARION: *No.*

ALFRED: *Well, since we're going to sleep together. I think it's only fair we should see you with your clothes off.*

EMILE: *It's only fair!*

MARION: *Why? We can meet later at the Neptuna. They've got*

' *Vera Cruz* ' on.

ALFRED turns to camera and smiles.

ALFRED to camera: *With my friend Burt Lancaster.*

EMILE: *No, we'll come with you to the Zodiac.*

DOMINIQUE: *No.*

ALFRED: *Yes.*

They all get up and leave.

Bright neon lights against a background of black.

MARION off: *No!*

EMILE off: *Yes!*

DOMINIQUE off: *No!*

ALFRED off: *Clothes off all women!*

MARION off: *No!*

EMILE off: *Yes!*

They all come into the Zodiac strip-tease club.

VOICE off: *Chéri-Bibi with Chéri-Bibi.*

COMPERE off: *You are about to discover all the sensual delights of the Amazon.*

VOICE off: *Oh, it's disgusting!*

VOICE off: *Well, it's all your friends' fault, what can you expect?*

EMILE, ALFRED and the two girls sit down at a table.

EMILE to DOMINIQUE: *When are you on?*

DOMINIQUE: *A quarter of an hour.*

ALFRED: *Hey, look at Angela!*

ANGELA is sitting at another table, talking to a strange MAN.

ANGELA smiling: *Do you come here often, sir?*

MAN: *No, not very often.*

ANGELA: *Do you like the show?*

MAN: *Yes, yes!*

ANGELA looks anxiously towards EMILE.

A girl, dressed all in feathers, is doing her act on the floor.

Cut to EMILE's table.

ALFRED nodding towards the performer: *She's hot stuff.*

ALFRED and EMILE laugh, noticing ANGELA's discomfort.

EMILE: *That's what I call community.*

ANGELA is furious.

ANGELA getting up and shouting to EMILE: *You disgust me!*

Again bright neon lights against a dark background.

ANGELA stands in front of a chemist shop.

ANGELA'S VOICE off: *In both comedies and tragedies, at the end of the third act, the heroine hesitates: her fate hangs in balance. It's what old Corneille and young Molière called suspense . . .*

ANGELA is back in her flat. She sits at the table, playing with a pair of scissors.

EMILE, in the bathroom, examines his face in the mirror. He pulls at his eyes to look Chinese.

He makes a buzzing noise, like a fly.

ANGELA gets up and walks towards him.

ANGELA: *Do you prefer me in pyjamas or a nightdress, sweetheart?*
EMILE: *Pyjamas.*
ANGELA walking back to the table: *No, I'll wear a nightdress, it's more convenient.*

She pulls out a nightdress from a cupboard.

EMILE off: Now *what have you been up to?*
ANGELA: *What have I been up to?*
EMILE off: *The soap's all squishy.*
ANGELA: *It's not squishy at all.*
EMILE off: *Yes, it's all squishy.*
ANGELA: *It's not in the least bit squishy.*
EMILE off: *If I tell you it's squishy . . . anyway . . . next time . . .*

EMILE is brushing his teeth.

EMILE: *You agree, Angela?*
ANGELA off: *Quite agree, darling, but I think . . .*
EMILE: *Poor fool! Anyway, I'm not speaking to you anymore.*

In the bedroom, EMILE and ANGELA are getting into bed.

EMILE: *We're not talking to one another?*
ANGELA: *No, we're not.*

EMILE turns off the standard lamp.

There is total darkness.

ANGELA'S VOICE: *My bottom's cold.*
EMILE'S VOICE: *We'd agreed we weren't speaking!*

EMILE turns on the standard lamp.

ANGELA gets up, picks up the standard lamp and carries it over to the bookshelf. She chooses a book and goes back to bed.

She covers part of the book with her hand and shows it to EMILE.

40

Close-up of book. The title reads: MONSTER!

EMILE gets out of bed, picks up the standard lamp and takes it to the bookshelf. He brings back a book on which he scribbles hurriedly with a pencil. He shows it to ANGELA. Close-up of the title which reads: EVA . . . GET STUFFED! They both get up and go to the bookshelf, choosing several books. Getting back into bed they show each other the following titles:

She: EXECUTIONER!

He: PERNICIOUS MUMMY!

She: SWINDLER!

He: SARDINE!

He: ALL WOMEN . . . TO THE STAKE!

A shot of ANGELA's balcony from outside. Daytime.

Inside the flat, ANGELA in her dressing-gown, walks towards the bathroom with a basin on her head.

She turns on the shower but the water does not run.

She goes to the living room and returns with a hammer.

She knocks on a pipe and the water begins to run.

ANGELA shouting: *What is it, I can't hear a thing!*

She picks up the hammer, knocks on the pipe and the water stops running.

She comes out of the bathroom.

NEIGHBOUR off: *Telephone, Madame Récamier.*

ANGELA: *Thanks, I'm coming.*

ANGELA sings to herself, goes through the front door and takes the telephone from her NEIGHBOUR.

ANGELA into telephone: *Hello? Who's calling?*

EMILE is in the bookshop, telephone in hand.

EMILE: *I'm calling!*

Resume on ANGELA at the telephone.

ANGELA: *Why, no kidding?* Pause. *Nothing, I said no kidding! No, I won't forgive you!* She covers the receiver and whispers. *Yes, I forgive you.* She puts the receiver to her ear again. *What? . . . Why did you . . .*

EMILE into telephone: *I didn't!*

ANGELA into telephone: *Yes, you did.*

EMILE into telephone: *No, I didn't.*

ANGELA into telephone: *When I begged you to give me a baby.*
EMILE into telephone: *I went. . . . Brrrrr?*
ANGELA into telephone: *Emile, I've suddenly thought of something.*
Shouting. *You're a big drag!*

She slams down the telephone.

Resume on EMILE in the bookshop. A MAN turns to him.

MAN: *Anything wrong, Monsieur Récamier?*
EMILE: *Oh, she can go cook an egg!*

ANGELA is breaking an egg into a frying pan.

She waltzes into the living room and lights a cigarette.

ANGELA singing: *Emile. . . . Alfred. . . . I have an ugly face, but a very pretty . . .*

NEIGHBOUR off: *Madame Récamier!*
ANGELA: *What is it now?*
NEIGHBOUR off: *Telephone!*
ANGELA: *Yes, I'm coming.*

She runs into the kitchen, picks up the frying pan and tosses the egg into the air.

She runs to the telephone, frying pan still in hand.

ANGELA into telephone: *Hello? Hello, Alfred . . . just a second.*

She runs back into the kitchen, holds out the frying pan and the egg drops down into it.

She returns to the telephone, the egg on a plate, and begins to eat.

ANGELA into telephone: *Hello? Yes, seriously, I'm listening.*

ALFRED is in a café, talking into the telephone.

ALFRED: *Well, here it is. . . . Something very important has come up! Yes . . . last night.*

ANGELA into telephone: *What? No kidding? . . . Nothing. I said no kidding! . . . No, not right away! . . . Because . . . not right away.*
ALFRED into telephone: *Okay. In half an hour. At Marcel's. . . . What? . . . I said okay. Don't you understand French?*

ANGELA is smiling and sitting by the telephone.

Resume on ALFRED, standing by the bar of the café.

JEANNE MOREAU stands next to him.

JEANNE MOREAU: *How's things?*
ALFRED: *And you? Things okay with Jules and Jim?*
JEANNE MOREAU: *Moderato!*

ANGELA comes down the staircase outside her flat.

SUZANNE is leaning against a wall, reading.

ANGELA: *Hi, Suzanne! Everything okay?*

SUZANNE: *No. I wanted to see you.*

ANGELA: *What's the book?*

SUZANNE stretches her hands forward and pretends to play a piano. Music off.

She then ' fires ' two shots with her fingers into the air.

ANGELA: *Ahh! ' Shoot the Pianist ' . . . did you see the film? Aznavour was super.*

SUZANNE: *I've got problems. They kicked me out of Simca's.*

Close shot of a man in working clothes, looking into camera. More shots of passing crowd in the street. Close-up of a man laughing. Shots of hurrying crowds and busy traffic.

ANGELA off: *Is that why you phoned me yesterday evening?*

SUZANNE off: *Yes. Do you think the Zodiac would hire me for a few days until something turns up?*

ANGELA off: *What about the Party? Can't they help?*

SUZANNE off: *Oh, they kicked me out too!*

ANGELA off: *No kidding?*

SUZANNE off: *They made a fuss because I got up too late on Sunday to sell l'Humanité! How much do you make in that streep-joint?*

ANGELA off: *Strip-joint.*

SUZANNE off: *No, streep-joint. It's not English, it's American!*

ANGELA off: *Oh, I thought . . .*

SUZANNE off: *No, I'm quite sure.*

ANGELA off: *Would you be embarrassed, getting undressed in front of strange men?*

SUZANNE off: *No . . . they're all a lot of creeps.*

ANGELA off: *Yes . . . that's how I feel.*

ANGELA and SUZANNE are walking along the street and laughing. More shots of people in the crowd; a newsboy at the tube entrance.

SUZANNE off: *How much can you make?*

ANGELA off: *3,000 francs a day.*

SUZANNE off: *Great . . . do you think they'd take me?*

ANGELA off: *You'd have to talk to Luciano, or else Bianchini. He was in yesterday, wanted some girls for Marseilles.*

SUZANNE off: *Oh, Marseilles, I know what that means. My friend Lola went off to Marseilles . . . next thing we knew, she was in*

Buenos-Aires!

ANGELA and SUZANNE are now standing at a crossing. They are laughing.

ANGELA: *Well then, see Luciano!*

They start walking. ANGELA lights a cigarette.

More shots of milling traffic and crowded streets.

SUZANNE off: *Damn! I forgot to tell you . . .*

ANGELA off: *What?*

SUZANNE off: *I bumped into Emile earlier. He told me to keep an eye on you.*

ANGELA off: *You? Why you?*

Close-up of two negroes walking along the street.

SUZANNE off: *I dunno! He's afraid you're going out with Alfred.*

ANGELA off: *But it's all over between you and Alfred, isn't it?*

SUZANNE off: *Sometimes I miss . . .*

More close-ups of faces in the crowd.

ANGELA off: *Alfred!*

ALFRED off: *Hi! How's things?*

SUZANNE off: *Alfred? No, but I liked his shoulders.*

ANGELA off: *The thing I like best about Emile . . . is his knees.*

SUZANNE off: *What can you do with knees?*

ANGELA off: *Keep your grip!*

Sound of laughter off.

Close-up of newsboy by the tube entrance.

ANGELA off: *Monsieur Luciano!*

SUZANNE off: *Who's he?*

A man approaches camera from across the street.

ANGELA off: *Oh, him! He watches the girls getting out of the swimming-pool.*

ANGELA and SUZANNE now stand outside the strip-tease club.

ANGELA: *Good luck!*

SUZANNE shaking her hand: *See you!*

Two quick close-ups of ANGELA: first she sits in the kitchen and looks pensive, then tears are streaming down her face.

ANGELA now enters a café.

She goes towards the bar where ALFRED is standing. He stretches out his hand. ANGELA takes off her glove with some difficulty and they shake hands.

44

ALFRED: *Hi, Angela!*

ANGELA: *Have you been here long, Alfred?*

ALFRED: *Me? No! Twenty-seven years. . . . What'll you have?*

ALFRED to BARMAN: *Hello.*

BARMAN: *Hello.*

ANGELA: *. . . A Dubonnet.*

They take their glasses and go to sit down at a corner table.

ANGELA: *Well, what shall we talk about?*

ALFRED: *I don't know, I'm scared.*

The BARMAN approaches, pours them a drink.

ALFRED takes the bottle from the BARMAN and puts it down on the table.

They sip their drinks; ALFRED lights a cigarette.

ALFRED: *Were you surprised I phoned this morning?*

ANGELA: *I'm not sure.*

ALFRED: *Were you pleased?*

ANGELA: *I'm not sure.*

ALFRED: *Well, what shall we talk about?*

ANGELA: *Dunno, I am trying to think of something.*

ALFRED: *There was a really funny story in Paris-Jour this morning . . .*

ANGELA taking off her coat: *What?*

ALFRED: *A girl was in love with two fellows at the same time. She sent them both express letters, arranging to meet one of them at the Gare du Nord, and the other one two hours later at the Port d'Italie.* ANGELA takes out a cigarette and lights it. *She put the letters in the post, and right after she'd posted them. . . . Pow, . . .* He bangs his forehead with his hand *. . . she realizes she's got the envelopes wrong. That the letter starting ' My darling Paul ' is in Pierre's envelope and vice versa. Well, she's quite frantic. She rushes over to the first bloke, the letter still hasn't arrived. The girl says to the fellow, ' Listen darling, you're going to receive an express letter . . . don't believe what it says '. He asks for an explanation and she's forced to tell him the whole story. In the end, he kicks her out for good. So the girl says to herself, ' I've lost one of them, but I can still keep the other one '. So she goes right across Paris and rushes over to the second fellow. The letter was already there. The second fellow doesn't seem at all angry, quite the contrary. So the girl says to him, ' You're a kind hearted guy, you've forgiven* *me '. He looks very surprised but doesn't say anything. So she tells the whole story all over again, because she thinks he's just keeping quiet to humiliate her before he really forgives her. Suddenly, the second fellow shows her the letter and kicks her out. Only then the girl discovers that she'd put them in the right envelopes after all.*

ANGELA: *Well, so what?*

ALFRED: *Nothing, I thought she sounded a bit like you.*

ANGELA: *Me? Nothing like me!*

ALFRED: *No? I don't mean the details, I mean her character . . . . A girl who's always making mistakes.*

He pours more drink into their glasses.

ANGELA: *No kidding?*

ALFRED: *Yes.*

He looks at her fixedly.

ANGELA: *Why are you looking at me like that?*

ALFRED: *Because I love you.*

ANGELA laughing: *Come on! Come off it!*

ALFRED: *Yes, Angela, I haven't slept all night. . . . I discovered it . . .*

ANGELA: *All alone?*

ALFRED: *Of course!*

ANGELA: *It's not true, is it?*

ALFRED: *Do you mind?*

ANGELA: *What if it's not true?*

ALFRED: *It is.*

ANGELA: *I don't know. . . . Yes, I suppose I do. . . . I don't know what's the matter. I'm always making mistakes. But one can't ever be sure.* She plays with her hair. *Let's try . . . tell me a lie.*

ALFRED looking out of the window: *It's raining!*

ANGELA: *Now, tell me the truth.*

ALFRED: *It's sunny.*

ANGELA: *Ahh!*

ALFRED: *What's the matter?*

ANGELA: *You're face doesn't change at all.*

ALFRED: *So what?*

ANGELA pensively: *Well, there ought to be a difference, because there's a difference between the truth and a lie!*

ALFRED reaching for a cigar: *I don't think it matters. . . . You just have to be able to tell!* He lights the cigar.

ANGELA: *Well, you know what you mean, but other people aren't*

46

obliged to believe you. . . . And it's a pity . . . because it means
that it's every man for himself.
ALFRED: *Oh, people always muddle through.*
ANGELA: *Yes, that's what's so sad.*
    ALFRED *pours them another drink.*
ALFRED: *Why don't you believe that I love you?*
ANGELA: *I'd like to be sure of it!*
ALFRED: *So would I.*
ANGELA: *You're not sure, Alfred?*
ALFRED: *I'm sure of me, yes, but not of you . . .*
ANGELA *laughing: Oh, that's all right then!*
ALFRED: *No, it's not all right.*
ANGELA: *Yes, it is, because it doesn't matter about me . . . whether*
I love you or not.
VOICE *off: Have pity for two poor blind men!*
ALFRED: *Oh, no. Not me, you don't!*
    Close shot of two MEN wearing dark glasses and carrying white
    canes. They stand at the table.
FIRST MAN: *Oh, sorry.*
SECOND MAN: *With these glasses on, you can't see a damn thing!*
    They both lower their glasses and recognize ALFRED.
    They wave to him and move off.
ALFRED: *Ciao!*
ANGELA: *Who are they, I've never seen them before?*
ALFRED: *We all worked together a couple of years ago. The one*
in the blue coat is called Albert. I'm very fond of him. Last year
he invented this great scheme. He relights his cigar and takes a
puff. *He wrote letters to all the pregnant women in his neighbour-*
hood saying, ' Send me 1,000 francs and I'll tell you whether it'll
be a boy or a girl. If I am wrong, I'll refund the money '. And, of
course, he was right about fifty percent of the time. It's a real
winner!
ANGELA *seriously: Well, I think it's disgusting!*
ALFRED: *No, it's perfectly honest. . . . Fifty percent of the time he*
was wrong and then he refunded their money.
    He fills their glasses again.
ANGELA: *All the same, it's not right.*
ALFRED: *Well, what I think is disgusting is to be with one fellow*
and to think about another.

ANGELA peevishly: *And I think that when people don't know what they're talking about . . . they should shut up. . . . Monsieur Alfred.*

ALFRED: *I know what I'm talking about. You're thinking about Emile.*

ANGELA: *No, I'm not.*

ALFRED: *Well, what can I do to convince you that I love you?*

ANGELA: *Have you got a twenty franc piece?*

ALFRED: *Do you want me to put on a record?*

ANGELA smiling: *Yes.*

ALFRED reaching in his pocket: *Okay. What do you want, Itsy-Bitsy?*

ANGELA: *No! Charles.*

ALFRED: *Aznavour?*

ANGELA: *Yes.*

ALFRED getting up and throwing a photograph on the table: *Look at this photo.*

> Close-up of a juke-box. A record flips on to the turn-table. We hear music and a Charles Aznavour song.
>
> ANGELA and ALFRED remain silent. He looks at her meaningfully. She looks sad.
>
> Cut to the turn-table going round and round.
>
> Close-up of the photograph on the table. It shows EMILE with a friend.
>
> Individual close-ups of ANGELA and ALFRED looking at each other.
>
> The record finishes.

ANGELA looking at the photo: *Who's the girl?*

ALFRED: *You can see, can't you?*

ANGELA: *Yes, I can see!*

ALFRED: *I asked you a question before and you haven't answered it.*

ANGELA: *What question?*

ALFRED pouring a drink from the bottle: *What do I have to do to convince you that I love you?*

ANGELA playfully: *Yes, what could you do?*

ALFRED: *If I were to crash my head into the wall, would you believe me?*

ANGELA: *I don't know whether to say ' of course ' or ' maybe '.*

ALFRED: *Here goes!*

> He gets up and leaves the table.
>
> Cut to ALFRED running across the street and banging his head

48

against a wall.

He runs back into the café and sits down at the table.

ANGELA: *I believe you.* She pauses and looks up. *Oh, it's one thirty, I've got to run.*

ALFRED picking up the bill: *Damn. . . . 300 francs. I haven't got enough.*

ANGELA: *Well, I haven't any money on me.*

She puts on her coat.

ALFRED: *Never mind, I've got an idea.*

He gets up and walks towards the bar.

ALFRED to BARMAN: *I'll ask you a question and you answer either 'yes' or 'no', okay?*

BARMAN: *Okay.*

ANGELA approaching: *Well, are we going?*

ALFRED to ANGELA: *Just a moment.* To BARMAN. *If you answer 'yes' I owe you ten thousand francs, and if you answer 'no' you owe me the money. Okay?*

BARMAN: *Okay.*

ALFRED: *Here's the question, 'Can you lend me ten thousand francs?'*

BARMAN wiping his hands on a towel: *No.*

ALFRED: *Then that's how much you owe me! . . . I'll pay you back next week.*

He waves to the BARMAN and follows ANGELA out.

In the street, ALFRED waits for a car to pass and crosses the road, catching up with ANGELA.

Only a close-up of ANGELA remains in frame.

ALFRED off: *Why don't you ever wait for me?*

ANGELA: *I must go and make lunch.*

ALFRED off: *Emile's lunch! Well, Angela. . . . Emile's lunch?*

ANGELA: *I'm just thinking.*

ALFRED off: *I don't know, Angela, but it's a bit much . . .*

ANGELA: *If in five minutes the blinds are still down, it'll mean that I'm coming back.*

ALFRED off: *And if they're up?*

ANGELA: *I shan't be back. It will mean that I've made it up with Emile.* To camera. *That I'm happy.*

EMILE and ANGELA are now outside her flat.

She walks up the staircase, and he goes to lean against a wall. Cut to view of the balcony. The two red blinds are up.

Cut to ALFRED, watching the balcony. He lights a cigarette. A workman comes past and takes a light from ALFRED's cigarette.

Resume on the balcony. One blind moves slowly down.

Resume on ALFRED, giving a light to another passing workman. Resume on the balcony. The second blind moves down and then quickly moves up again.

Resume on ALFRED, giving a light to one more passer-by. He is still leaning against the wall, looking up. Only the butt of the cigarette remains in his hand. He throws it away in disgust. Resume on the balcony. Both blinds are now down but they quickly move up again, one by one.

ANGELA off: *I want to be alone! Do I have to say it in Chinese?*

EMILE off: *Angela!*

EMILE and ANGELA are in the hall of their flat.

ANGELA producing the photograph: *What about this photo?*

EMILE putting it in his pocket: *But that's an old story . . . why bother about it?*

ANGELA: *If you want to be forgiven you might at least kiss me!*

EMILE: *You kiss me.*

ANGELA: *I want a baby!*

EMILE: *No, don't start that again.*

ANGELA: *I'm not starting it again . . . just continuing!*

EMILE: *Well, don't continue!*

ANGELA: *I'm not continuing, I'm starting it again.*

EMILE walking away: *Stupid bitch!*

They look at each other, pause and run to kiss.

ANGELA and EMILE are now sitting on the stairs.

ANGELA: *I want a baby.*

EMILE: *Don't be indecent, Angela!*

ANGELA: *Don't be cruel, Emile!*

EMILE: *That plaid skirt really doesn't suit you at all!*

ANGELA: *That's all right. I don't* want *people to fancy me.*

She gets up and pauses.

EMILE and ANGELA embrace and then quickly move apart.

ANGELA: *I want a baby!*

EMILE: *Stop acting the fool.*

ANGELA: *Right, I'm going to the Zodiac.*
EMILE: *That's it, take your clothes off in front of three dozen strangers! You disgust me!*
ANGELA: *Poor creep! If you think we can live on your lousy money. . . . You're such a coward, Emile!*
EMILE: *I'd rather be a coward than an idiot!*
ANGELA: *Why am I an idiot just because I want a baby?*
EMILE: *If you don't shut up, I shall go!*
    He walks out of frame.
ANGELA: *Where'd you go?*
EMILE coming back into frame: *I dunno. . . . Mexico.*
ANGELA: *You're mad!*
EMILE: *No, you're mad.*
ANGELA: *I want a baby!*
    He throws up his hands in despair and walks off.

    In the street, EMILE approaches a strange MAN; ANGELA is close by.
EMILE to MAN: *Excuse me, sir! Sorry to trouble you, but could you possibly spare a few minutes to give this young lady a baby?*
MAN: *Oh!*
    Cut to EMILE approaching another stranger.
    His question is not heard but the MAN replies.
MAN: *Oh, no, really, it's a bit early in the day . . . and, anyway, I haven't got the time.*
    ANGELA runs out of frame.
    EMILE walks into the Zodiac.
EMILE to BARMAN: *Hello!*
BARMAN pouring out a drink: *Hello!*
EMILE: *Is Angela here?*
BARMAN: *She's on after Dominique.*
EMILE: *Thanks.*
    He walks towards the floor and sits down at a table.
    DOMINIQUE is doing her act.
    EMILE is watching closely.
    DOMINIQUE is in a further state of undress.
    EMILE is still watching.
    DOMINIQUE, naked to the waist and covering her breast with her hands, is walking off.

51

EMILE to approaching WAITRESS: *Is Angela on soon?*
WAITRESS: *No. She's left.*
EMILE: *Why? Damn!* To passing MAN. *Silly creep!*
MAN: *Creep, yourself!*

Close-up of EMILE in profile. He smokes a cigarette.

TITLE in large letters on a black background:
EMILE IS SO UNHAPPY, HE DOESN'T CARE A DAMN.

EMILE is now walking along the street. He stops to greet passers-by. He says hello to the two BLIND MEN. He walks towards a PROSTITUTE, who takes him into her doorway.

EMILE, wearing his undershirt, is now in the PROSTITUTE'S room.

EMILE: *Thus, it is quite involuntarily that people commit an injustice. . . . They are unjust and cruel.*
PROSTITUTE from her bed: *Oh, quite involuntarily, in my opinion.*
EMILE: *They are unjust and cruel.*

ANGELA stands by a parked car, outside ALFRED's flat. She adjusts her stocking, pats her hair and moves forward. She slowly walks up the stairs, pauses to take off her coat and knocks on ALFRED's door. She crosses herself quickly before the door opens.

Close shot of EMILE, walking along the street.

NEWSBOY off: *France-Soir, Paris-Presse, Le Monde, Marie-Claire!*

EMILE knocks on his NEIGHBOUR's door.

EMILE: *I want to telephone.*

The NEIGHBOUR opens the door and hands him a telephone.

EMILE begins to dial.

A MAN leaves the NEIGHBOUR's flat, passing EMILE.

NEIGHBOUR to MAN: *'Bye darling!*

EMILE into telephone: *Hello? Hello, sir. This is Emile Récamier. Could you see if Alfred Lubitsch is home?*

Cut to an elderly man opening his french window, and walking along a balcony roof to ALFRED's french window. He runs back.

Resume on EMILE at the telephone.

EMILE into telephone: *. . . Tell him I'm going to Mexico.*

Resume on the elderly man, moving once again along the roof balcony to ALFRED's french window.

Cut to ALFRED at his window, receiving the message. He goes back to sit on the bed, next to ANGELA. She is sitting in her slip, pretending to read. ALFRED plays with her hair. (*Still*)

ALFRED: *Why Mexico?*

ANGELA looking up: *It's not fair. It's always when you're with people that you're not with them, and vice versa.*

ALFRED: *Meaning what?*

ANGELA getting up and dressing: *Meaning, I'm off to Mexico.*

As she leaves ALFRED's flat, she crosses herself once again.

NEWSBOY off: *Paper ... France-Soir, Paris-Presse, Le Monde, Marie-Claire. ... Paper. ... Figaro Littéraire.*

Close-up of ANGELA, singing under a red light.

ANGELA singing:

> *I can be a bad girl,*
> *I can be a pest,*
> *But the men never complain*
> *'Cos I look good undressed.*

Cut to ANGELA sitting on the stairs, outside her front door. She plays with her keys and seems undecided.

The NEIGHBOUR's boyfriend comes up the stairs. She gets up quickly and goes to open her door. She goes inside.

EMILE is reading a newspaper.

ANGELA takes off her beret and hangs it up.

She moves into the living room; he goes towards her. She turns round and walks by the table, only to meet him face to face. She turns again, walks back, and they meet again. She walks to the wall and stands with her back to camera. Finally she turns round.

ANGELA: *I don't know what to say.*

EMILE: *Just say the truth.*

He moves past her.

ANGELA: *I was at Alfred's. ... I went to bed with him.*

EMILE: *I don't believe you. . . . I don't believe you. . . . I don't believe you!*

ANGELA: *I did.*

EMILE: *But why, for heaven's sake?*

ANGELA: *To have a baby. . . . Because you didn't want to.*

EMILE: *Are you having me on, Angela?*

53

ANGELA: *Maybe.*

EMILE strokes her neck; ANGELA begins to unzip her dress. EMILE walks away.

EMILE: *I'm not sure if it's a comedy or a tragedy.* To camera. *But in any case it's a masterpiece.*

ANGELA taking off her shoes: *He put on an Aznavour record. . . . You know the one that always makes me feel like jelly. It begins ta, ta, ti, ta . . .*

EMILE: *No, it begins ti, ti, tati . . .*

He moves towards her. The screen goes black.

ANGELA off: *No, it's not ta, ta, ta. It's tata, ti . . .*

EMILE off: *No, it's not ti, ti. It's ti, ti, ta, ta . . .*

ANGELA switches on the side light. They are in the bedroom, taking off their slippers. They get into bed; ANGELA sets the alarm clock, folds her hands, saying a silent prayer.

ANGELA turning to EMILE: *Shall I put the light out?*

EMILE: *Yes.*

ANGELA: *It's sad.*

EMILE: *Yes, it's sad.*

He turns his head away from her. The screen becomes black.

ANGELA off: *I'm sorry, love.*

EMILE off: *I'm not talking to you.*

ANGELA turns on the standard lamp, picks it up and walks with it to the bookshelf. EMILE follows her. They pick out some books and return to bed.

ANGELA turns on the side light and shows him a book.

ANGELA: *Can't you tell, you idiot?. . . If you don't love me. . . .*

She points to the book title: I STILL LOVE YOU.

EMILE: *And what if you're pregnant?*

ANGELA: *Yes, it's terrible!*

EMILE: *I've suddenly got an idea.*

ANGELA: *Me too.*

EMILE: *It's very simple.*

ANGELA: *We won't know for several . . .*

EMILE: *. . . days, whether you really are . . .*

ANGELA: *. . . pregnant . . .*

EMILE: *And to be quite sure . . .*

ANGELA: *You suggest giving me a baby . . . so . . .*

EMILE: *. . . that I'll be sure . . .*

ANGELA: . . . *either way . . . of being . . .*
EMILE: . . . *the father.*
ANGELA: *Okay, let's go!*
TITLE in large letters on a black background:
ONCE IT WAS OVER, ANGELA TURNED ON THE LIGHT.

ANGELA and EMILE are still in bed. (*Still*)
EMILE: *That was a close thing!*
ANGELA: *Why are you laughing?*
EMILE: *Because you're awful, Angela!*
ANGELA: *I'm not awful, I'm just a woman!*
They laugh together. ANGELA turns off the light.

THE END

A MARRIED WOMAN

CREDITS:

Production Company	Anouchka Films/Orsay Films (Paris)
Production Manager	Philippe Dussart
Director	Jean-Luc Godard
Assistant Directors	Claude Othnin-Girard
	Jean-Pierre Léaud
	Hélène Kalouguine
Script	Jean-Luc Godard
Director of Photography	Raoul Coutard
Camera Operator	Georges Liron
Editor	Agnès Guillemot
	Françoise Collin
Art Director	Henri Nogaret
Jazz Music	Claude Nougaro
Song ' Quand le film est triste '	J. D. Loudermilk
	G. Aber
	L. Morisse
Sung by	Sylvie Vartan
Sound	Antoine Bonfanti
	René Levert
	Jacques Maumont

CAST:

Charlotte Giraud	Macha Méril
Roberto, the Lover	Bernard Noël
Pierre, the Husband	Philippe Leroy
Roger Leenhardt	Roger Leenhardt
Madame Céline	Rita Maiden
Nicolas	Chris Tophe
Two girls in swimming-pool bar	Margaret Le-Van
	Véronique Duval

A MARRIED WOMAN

Brief credits appear on the screen.

TITLE:

FRAGMENTS OF A FILM MADE IN 1964

The title cuts and the screen remains white.

CHARLOTTE's left hand, wearing a wedding ring, slides into frame until it is visible to the elbow.

We realize the whiteness is that of a sheet, covering a bed.

The camera is shooting from a high angle.

CHARLOTTE off: *I don't know.*

ROBERT's hand appears and slides towards CHARLOTTE's.

ROBERT off: *You don't know if you love me?*

CHARLOTTE off: *Why do you keep talking? It's so nice like this.*

CHARLOTTE now sits upright. Her back is bare.

ROBERT off: *What's that, there?*

CHARLOTTE bending her head: *Oh, that was when I was little . . .*

ROBERT's hand comes from below and travels up her back. Their two hands caress each other on her shoulder.

CHARLOTTE: *Once, by the seaside, I fell over.*

CHARLOTTE, seen in profile, is sitting naked on the bed.

In front of her are ROBERT's hairy legs. (*Still*)

ROBERT off: *Really, you can't go very far in love.*

CHARLOTTE: *How d'you mean. . . . I don't understand?*

ROBERT off: *Yes, you kiss someone, you caress them, but really you remain outside. . . . It's like a house you never go into.*

CHARLOTTE: *But you can melt into somebody if you love them.*

ROBERT off: *Yes, but you are inside people at other times. When you are not thinking, when there is nothing special about the occasion.*

CHARLOTTE stretching out her hands: *I love you.*

ROBERT's hands come into frame and take CHARLOTTE's.

Close-up of CHARLOTTE, facing camera. The lower edge of the frame reaches the beginning of her breasts.

ROBERT's two hands move slowly towards her neck.

ROBERT off: *You ought to do like they do in Italian films. . . . Have you seen any? The women don't shave under their arms.*

CHARLOTTE: *I prefer American films, Hollywood ones . . . they're prettier.*

ROBERT off: *Yes, but they arouse one less.*

The music played during the credits begins again. It is Beethoven's Quartet No. 10 — the leitmotif of the film.

CHARLOTTE's bare leg is on the sheet. ROBERT's hand caresses her thigh. We see shots of CHARLOTTE's legs from different angles.

CHARLOTTE off: *You've got nice eyebrows.*

She puts her legs over ROBERT's, which now appear in frame.

ROBERT off: *Do you think so?*

CHARLOTTE off: *Do you know that in Japan it's the most important thing?*

Her hand grasps the sheet and covers her bare legs with it. ROBERT's hand pushes back the sheet.

ROBERT off: *Why don't you like me to look at you?*

Large close-up of CHARLOTTE's stomach. ROBERT's hands caress it, near the navel.

ROBERT off: *I'd like to have a child by you.*

CHARLOTTE off: *I've got one already.*

ROBERT off: *You told me it was by another marriage?*

CHARLOTTE off: *Yes.*

ROBERT off: *Was your husband married long, the first time?*

CHARLOTTE off: *No, his wife left him after two months. . . . She went off with the manager of a casino in Djibouti.*

CHARLOTTE's bare legs wave in the air.

CHARLOTTE singing off:

> *Where have all the flowers gone?*
> *Long time passing.*
> *Where have all the flowers gone?*
> *Long, long ago.*

Close-up of ROBERT's back. CHARLOTTE, who is facing him, can scarcely be seen. Her hands caress the back of his neck. (*Still*)

ROBERT: *When are we going to live together? It's been three months now.*

CHARLOTTE: *I told you. . . . Not until I'm divorced. Things don't move so quickly.*

ROBERT: *You promise? . . . You've spoken to him?*

CHARLOTTE: *Yes.*

ROBERT: *I love your teeth.*

CHARLOTTE's bare legs on the sheet are seen from above.

ROBERT off: *Take it off.*

CHARLOTTE off: *No.*

ROBERT off: *Yes.*

Cut to low angle shot of a plane passing in the sky.

Resume on CHARLOTTE's legs.

CHARLOTTE off: *I'm cold.*

ROBERT off: *Let me look at you.*

Close-up of CHARLOTTE, facing camera. ROBERT's hand strokes her cheek. She takes the hand and kisses the palm.

CHARLOTTE: *I love you.*

ROBERT off: *I love you too.*

Close-up of CHARLOTTE in profile.

CHARLOTTE: *Do you love me?*

ROBERT off: *Yes.*

High angle shot of CHARLOTTE's face. She is lying down, and her head is thrown back.

CHARLOTTE shaking her head: *Yes . . . yes . . . yes . . . yes. . . . Oh, yes!*

Her face now looks ecstatic.

CHARLOTTE: *Yes . . .*

Close-up of the cover of a Gallimard book, ' The Nylon Age — The Soul — Elsa Triolet '. The news is heard on a radio.

ANNOUNCER off: *There is a large amount of traffic on the roads. Twelve million French people have already left the towns, fascinated by the sea and the sun. . . . Two hundred thousand police have been appointed by the authorities for the task of controlling this massive exodus.* Close-up of a transistor radio on a table. *At 2.30 there had already been twenty-three people killed and a hundred and thirty-two injured. So far, these are the total casualties for the public holiday, which the traffic experts have already predicted will have a particularly high accident rate.*

CHARLOTTE leafs through the book and shuts it.

She is sitting on the bed, still naked. She points to something outside the frame.

61

CHARLOTTE: *Who's that? . . . Molière?*
ROBERT off: *Yes.*

Close-up of a portrait of Molière, hanging on the wall.

COMMENTARY off: *In 1694 Bossuet published his* Maxims and Reflections on the Theatre: '*I believe that it has been sufficiently proved that the representation of agreeable passions on the stage inclines the viewer to sin, if only by employing images calculated to arouse lust.' Molière replied that the theatre helps to protect the viewer from sin, by purifying love.* Quick shot of CHARLOTTE in profile, then resume on the portrait. *When he was at last alone with Mademoiselle Molière who could not prevent herself from crying, he looked at her a long time without speaking. His rather too large blue eyes, which were always extremely benign in expression, had something in them which might be interpreted as a very gentle reproach. He looked like a small boy who is being made to suffer, and cannot understand why. Nevertheless, the real child was the kneeling young woman, who had such an innocent air. . . .* Resume on CHARLOTTE, still naked on the bed. She has picked up Elsa Triolet's book again . . . *and who could do so much harm.*

ROBERT off: *Well, Princess, how do you do?*
CHARLOTTE: *I must get dressed.*
ROBERT off: *We've got plenty of time, Charlotte.*
CHARLOTTE putting down her book: *No, and besides, I don't want to now.*

ROBERT comes out of the bathroom and is about to take down a shirt which is hanging on a door. He is in a vest and pants. Around his waist can be seen a belt which keeps a flat, black, rectangular box in place on his stomach.

ROBERT: *Are you going home this evening?*
CHARLOTTE off, going to the bathroom: *No, but the maid has the day off and so I have to fetch our kid from school.*

ROBERT goes towards her. She is now in her panties, her arms hiding her breasts.

ROBERT dressing: *Well, how do you like the apartment?*
CHARLOTTE: *Let me just have a look.* She goes out of the room to look around the apartment. *Was it expensive?*
ROBERT: *One thousand three hundred francs. . . . But that's the furniture as well.*

ROBERT walks around the room and lights a cigarette.

CHARLOTTE off: *I think that's expensive, if all it means is we can't get thrown out.*

ROBERT: *You know, you can get onto the roof as well.*

CHARLOTTE crosses the little kitchen.

CHARLOTTE: *How d'you do that?* She opens a door. *Out here?*

ROBERT off: *At the end of the corridor, there is a little staircase.*

CHARLOTTE disappears. He comes in and rushes after her in a rage.

ROBERT: *Charlotte, what the hell are you up to? You must be nuts going out like that!*

Outside. CHARLOTTE goes down the stairs onto the roof. (*Still*) She is still in her panties and almost dances, hiding her breasts with her arms.

CHARLOTTE: *Why should I? Don't you know Fantomas?*

ROBERT shouting off: *Come back at once!*

CHARLOTTE in mock innocence: *I thought you liked me with no clothes on.*

She comes back.

They are now both walking around the flat.

ROBERT: *Look, don't put words into my mouth.*

CHARLOTTE: *Listen, I've got my husband all day, I don't want the same thing all over again when I'm with you.*

They go back into the bedroom.

ROBERT: *Go on! Get dressed! and stop talking about him all the time.*

CHARLOTTE: *I'm not, you are.*

ROBERT: *You're right . . . sorry!*

CHARLOTTE passes in front of the portrait of Molière, and picks up a bra from a chair, looking at a point on the opposite wall.

CHARLOTTE: *And who are those two on the mirror?*

ROBERT: *It's Dullin and Louis Jouvet.*

CHARLOTTE: *And from behind . . .* Sound of the bell in ROBERT's stomach-belt . . . *is that love too? No, that's vice. . . . But it doesn't matter.*

ROBERT off: *You're dreadful. Each time you use my razor you never clean it afterwards.*

CHARLOTTE: *Don't keep telling me I'm a slut.*

ROBERT comes back into frame. She turns round, holding the fastening of her bra at the back.

ROBERT: *I never said that.*

CHARLOTTE: *Please help me . . . I can't do it.* He tries clumsily to do up the bra. *It's not my fault if I have to rush off. . . . On Tuesday it was you.*

ROBERT: *Yes, of course, I had to. I was going to rehearsals at the Sarah Bernhardt.*

CHARLOTTE: *You don't believe me when I tell you I'm going to fetch the kid from school.*

ROBERT: *Yes, I believe you.*

CHARLOTTE: *Ouch! Careful!*

ROBERT: *Wait, wait . . .*

He manages at last to fix her bra. She turns to face him and thanks him with a kiss. She then looks in surprise at the black box which he has strapped on by a belt over his vest.

CHARLOTTE: *Whatever is that?*

ROBERT: *It's a French invention, perfected by Swiss specialists.* He walks up and down in front of her. *It makes one stand straight. The mechanism is regulated in such a way that the slightest pressure exerted on it by an incorrect posture sets off an alarm signal.*

CHARLOTTE: *It sounds good. . . . Can I have it?*

ROBERT goes into another room. She follows him.

We see a large close-up of a text:

THE INTIMATE DESIRES WHICH YOU DON'T DARE ADMIT. The camera pans from letter to letter, while they continue to talk, off.

ROBERT off: *Yes, I've got others. It's from a Lyons business man that I know. . . . I get to know a lot of people in the theatre. . . . He asked me to demonstrate it once in a while.*

CHARLOTTE off: *Isn't there a smaller one?*

ROBERT off: *Yes, but this is the de luxe model.*

Resume on CHARLOTTE. She is still in her panties and bra, but she has the special belt round her waist.

She goes towards a large wall-mirror which has the two portraits of Jouvet and Dullin stuck on it.

CHARLOTTE looking at the belt: *May I keep it?*

ROBERT coming into frame: *It's worth seven thousand francs.*

CHARLOTTE: *I'll give it to you tomorrow.* Pause. *If it's made to make one stand up properly, it must develop the bust.*

ROBERT: *Oh, yes!*

64

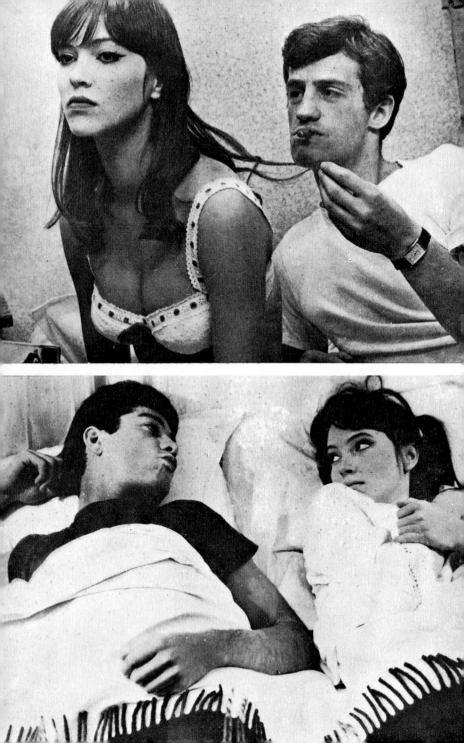

They embrace and hug each other. While she is kissing ROBERT's neck, her eyes look around for something.

CHARLOTTE: *Now, where did you put my stockings?*

Close-up of CHARLOTTE's hands fixing her suspenders.

COMMENTARY off: *Embrace, kiss. We stay silent. It was summer. Perhaps he has forgotten. Jealousy. When does he come back? This dress is pretty. I will tell you. It's dangerous. But you're not listening. Libertty Pleasure. To see nothing. Why this question? I was afraid to be late. Life in general.*

During the commentary we see the following close-ups of CHARLOTTE: her suspenders; her bra-fastener, badly done up; her hands putting it right; her bust in the bra; she buttons up her shirt-waist dress; her hands do up her skirt.

In the kitchen, CHARLOTTE looks at her watch and puts it to her ear.

CHARLOTTE: *What are you thinking?*

ROBERT is by the bedside table. He puts on his trousers and buttons them up.

ROBERT: *You know . . . you ought to talk to him again. He doesn't believe you. When does he get back?*

CHARLOTTE off: *I want what you want. You know that.*

Close-up of CHARLOTTE.

ROBERT off: *Well, do it then.*

Resume on ROBERT combing his hair in the kitchen; he turns round. Quick shot of CHARLOTTE near the door of the kitchen, then back to ROBERT.

ROBERT off: *Charlotte, what's this?* Pause as he mimes something which we do not see. *It's a Volkswagen turning to the right.*

CHARLOTTE: *Not before Saturday . . . or perhaps Friday . . . if he comes back on Friday!*

ROBERT coming into the kitchen: *In other words, three more days!*

CHARLOTTE is next to him, making herself up.

CHARLOTTE: *Oh look! If you've loved me for three months, you really must be able to wait another three days!*

ROBERT: *You're putting on too much powder.*

CHARLOTTE: *I'm doing what I like.*

ROBERT: *It's odd. Women live only for men, and yet they do nothing for them.*

73

CHARLOTTE picks up her handbag and they go towards the corridor.

CHARLOTTE: *Well, I really must go. Where are you parked?*

ROBERT puts on his jacket.

ROBERT: *In front of the tobacconist.*

CHARLOTTE: *You're not allowed to park there. Aren't you afraid of being caught?*

ROBERT: *There's always a way round it.*

CHARLOTTE: *Pierre says it's impossible.*

ROBERT shrugging his shoulders: *Oh yes, there's always a way of buying off the police.*

They go out. The door bangs shut behind them and the safety catch clicks home.

We are now outside a large block of apartments.

CHARLOTTE and ROBERT come out. CHARLOTTE looks cautiously both ways, while ROBERT runs off and drives back in an open car. CHARLOTTE dives in, sinking down in order not to be seen. The car will not start, so ROBERT has to push it a few yards. At last, the car starts.

Cut to a close-up of a neon sign:

TODAY AND TOMORROW.

Over this we hear the commentary.

COMMENTARY off: *In the middle of the corridor, hope . . . the image of a young girl. Who am I? I've never known exactly. The verb to follow, other reasons. I was once. Not here, a year ago. Only once, wasn't it? It's his fault. Always dream and then reality. A bitter satisfaction. I shall come back tomorrow. Friday or Saturday. He was afraid of me. I know he loves me. It's difficult. I'm on holiday. As the days go by. We met by chance. Happiness. I don't know.*

Inside the car, ROBERT and CHARLOTTE are seen from behind. He is driving; she is still slumped in the seat beside him, her knees against the dashboard. She glances through a newspaper.

The car moves along by the Seine.

ROBERT: *Are you ashamed to be seen with me?*

CHARLOTTE: *No, why Robert?*

ROBERT: *Well, sit up.*

CHARLOTTE: *I'm very comfortable like this. And anyway, it's the ideal position when you're at the cinema.*

ROBERT: *Well, what are you going to do this evening?*

CHARLOTTE: *This evening? Well, I'll do the dishes, and then I must tidy out the cupboards. Once Nicholas is in bed, I don't know. I'll watch television . . . we've got a super T.V. The technique of refrigeration in the service of aviation. Tele-Avia.*

As he is driving, ROBERT's hand strokes CHARLOTTE's knees.

ROBERT: *I'll telephone you, if you like?*

CHARLOTTE: *No . . . you always start to cry on the telephone. I don't want you to.*

Various close-up shots of the nude Maillol statues in the Tuileries as the commentary begins again.

COMMENTARY off: *Paris pleure après qu'il a plu mais plaira-t-il après qu'il a plu?*

Resume on ROBERT and CHARLOTTE as they drive through Paris.

CHARLOTTE: *Which way are you going?*

ROBERT: *By La Nation.*

CHARLOTTE: *Oh good, then you can drop me at the Printemps.*

ROBERT: *That's not the way to the Printemps.*

While they are talking, CHARLOTTE lifts herself slightly and turns the car mirror towards her to do her hair. He puts it back. She insists on having it her way.

CHARLOTTE: *Yes, there's a Printemps-Nation now. Didn't you know? They've got a fantastic bra counter.*

ROBERT: *I'll come with you, if you like.*

CHARLOTTE: *No, don't bother.*

ROBERT: *It's no bother. I haven't got anything to do before five.*

CHARLOTTE: *No. I said no. Have you never been married before?*

ROBERT: *No, not very many times. Why are you always asking me that?*

CHARLOTTE: *I wonder if you'll have me followed by a private detective if I deceive you when we're married.*

ROBERT: *There's no reason, just because all the men you know would do something so low, so unpleasant, to think I'm that type, too.*

Inserts of close-ups of a series of perfume names, which pass down the screen:

CRESCENDO
MY SIN
ARPEGE
SCANDAL
RUMEUR
PRETEXTE

Meanwhile the commentary begins again.

COMMENTARY off: *Lost illusions. When I was at school, it didn't matter.*

The car arrives in the Place de la Nation, where there is heavy traffic. CHARLOTTE gets out.

ROBERT: *Well, I'll see you tomorrow at the cinema . . . oh, yes!*

CHARLOTTE makes a friendly sign to him from a distance. The car disappears and she turns and runs towards the shop. Pan up to show the name Printemps-Nation.

High angle shot of the shop interior as CHARLOTTE moves between the counters.

She next runs along the pavement in the Rue Chausée-d'Antin, looking for a taxi. Behind her, a boarding shows the giant torso of a woman in a bra.

CHARLOTTE runs through a square, in front of the church of the Trinity, towards the taxi-rank. Before getting in, she turns to make sure that she is not being followed.

Close-up of the taxi-meter, as the ' For Hire ' sign is turned off. CHARLOTTE sinks down inside the taxi, and looks out of the back window.

COMMENTARY off: *Some time ago, when I was a secretary, you 'phoned I the person, I can't tell a lie. No, it's impossible. Yes, tomorrow, by the Madeleine, sometimes in the cinema. I find that disagreeable. I like that. Let me kiss you. In any case . . .*

CHARLOTTE to the driver: *Please stop, Monsieur.*

TAXI-DRIVER off: *We're not at the Champs-Elysées yet.*

CHARLOTTE: *That doesn't matter, stop.*

TAXI-DRIVER: *Here?*

CHARLOTTE irritably: *Yes. Yes, here!*

She gets out, pays the driver and crosses the road. (*Still*)

Cut to CHARLOTTE in another road: she looks from right to

left, then plunges into another taxi marked DS. Cut to yet another road. A taxi marked GZ 403 stops. CHARLOTTE gets out of it and goes towards a man who is holding a little boy by the hand.

CHARLOTTE: *Hello, Nicholas!*

NICHOLAS: *Hello.*

CHARLOTTE thanks the man who holds out NICHOLAS's briefcase, then gets NICHOLAS inside the taxi which starts off again. From above, we see the taxi move off down the street.

There is the sound of aeroplane engines. CHARLOTTE and NICHOLAS arrive on the airfield. They watch the plane land. The engines stop. The pilot, CHARLOTTE's husband, PIERRE, comes down from the plane and NICHOLAS runs towards him. A man and a secretary follow PIERRE out of the plane.

PIERRE: *Hello, son!*

He goes up to CHARLOTTE and stands beside her.

PIERRE: *Hello, darling! Aren't you going to kiss me?*

CHARLOTTE: *Yes.*

They kiss furtively, while NICHOLAS plays around them.

PIERRE: *What's the matter? Are you sulking?*

CHARLOTTE: *Not at all.*

PIERRE: *We went to Berlin and then we made a big detour.*

He does the introductions as the man joins them.

PIERRE: *Monsieur Leenhardt . . . my wife . . .*

LEENHARDT shaking her hand: *How do you do, Madame?* He points at the child. *That's your little boy?*

CHARLOTTE: *Yes.*

The camera stays with CHARLOTTE and LEENHARDT, as PIERRE and his son move away.

CHARLOTTE: *I was told that you made a big detour.*

LEENHARDT: *The reason for that was that I asked him to come with me to Auschwitz. I wanted to see a session of the trial. Have you heard of Auschwitz?*

The secretary is seen behind them, carrying a portfolio.

CHARLOTTE: *Oh, yes. Thalidomide?*

LEENHARDT: *Well, not exactly. It's an old story . . .*

CHARLOTTE: *Why yes, of course, Hitler!*

The camera follows PIERRE towards a mechanic, standing outside a hangar, as LEENHARDT answers:

LEENHARDT off: *Recently in Germany, I said to someone, ' Supposing tomorrow they were to kill all the Jews and all the hairdressers? '* Resumes on LEENHARDT and CHARLOTTE. *He replied . . . ' Why hairdressers? '*

CHARLOTTE: *Well, why the hairdressers?*

PIERRE off: *Have you got a car?*

LEENHARDT: *I thought of getting a taxi.*

PIERRE: *Certainly not. You'll come in with us.*

LEENHARDT: *In that case, I can't refuse.*

PIERRE: *Right, come along.*

LEENHARDT: *Yes. Thank you.*

> LEENHARDT reads a newspaper, as he and the secretary follow CHARLOTTE and PIERRE, while NICHOLAS plays around his parents. CHARLOTTE and PIERRE stay in frame as they talk to each other.

PIERRE: *Did you miss me?*

CHARLOTTE: *Yes, a lot.*

PIERRE: *I missed you.*

CHARLOTTE: *Is that true, Pierre?* A pause. *Why do you always ask such silly questions?*

PIERRE: *You're okay?*

CHARLOTTE: *Okay.*

PIERRE: *Did you finally get your driving licence?*

CHARLOTTE: *No.*

PIERRE: *Well, even if you haven't learned to drive yet, I hope your conduct elsewhere has been satisfactory?*

CHARLOTTE: *Oh, and what does that mean?*

PIERRE: *Nothing.*

CHARLOTTE: *You might have written to me. I never know where you are.*

PIERRE: *I never know where I'm going. What have you done today?*

CHARLOTTE: *Today? Mmm . . . let me see. . . . I did the washing-up with Raymonde because she was taking such ages. Then I tidied the cupboards. What else have I done? I telephoned Jeanette at the paper . . . and then I went to fetch Nicholas.*

> PIERRE takes a note out of his pocket and holds it up in front of his son.

PIERRE: *Do you want a dollar?*

NICHOLAS jumping with joy: *Ooh, yes please!*

LEENHARDT joins them as they reach the parked car.

PIERRE takes out his keys.

PIERRE to LEENHARDT: *Are you having dinner with us tonight?*

LEENHARDT getting into the car: *I'll have to call at the hotel first. That's very kind of you. Very kind.*

At home, CHARLOTTE is sitting at her dressing-table, wearing a slip. She plucks her eyebrows. On the table is a transistor radio with a large aerial.

PIERRE off: *Did you think about me?*

CHARLOTTE turns in the direction of his voice, and makes a W with her fingers near one eye, which she winks for a moment. (*Still*)

CHARLOTTE: *Pierre, do you know what that is?*

PIERRE off, in a convinced tone: *A Volkswagen turning to the right.*

CHARLOTTE: *You knew?*

PIERRE off: *No, I thought it out.* A pause. *We ought to hurry up. Come on.*

CHARLOTTE powdering her face: *You needn't have invited him.*

PIERRE off: *Why not? He's very intelligent.*

CHARLOTTE: *I didn't say he wasn't intelligent. . . . I only said you needn't have invited him.*

PIERRE off: *You needn't have told Madame Céline to go to the cinema.*

We now see PIERRE who is just finishing dressing. He has one foot up on the bed to do up his shoelace. Behind him, a photograph of himself in pilot's uniform is pinned to the wall.

CHARLOTTE off: *You need only find another maid.*

PIERRE standing upright: *You need only buy the Figaro.*

CHARLOTTE off: *You need only go out instead of me.*

A pause. Resume on CHARLOTTE as he looks at her.

PIERRE off: *Okay, I'll go. Ought I to buy leeks? On Radio Luxembourg they say that they lower the level of cholesterol in the blood . . .*

CHARLOTTE goes towards the bay window to put on her lipstick.

CHARLOTTE: *Right . . . leeks.*

PIERRE comes up to her and lifts up her slip.

PIERRE: *Oh, you've got new panties. They're nicer than the other ones.*

CHARLOTTE shrugging her shoulders: *They're just the same.*

PIERRE knots his tie, goes towards the bathroom and comes back, combing his hair.

PIERRE: *Oh no. The other ones looked like American army surplus.*

CHARLOTTE: *It's the American army now. It used to be the Russians.*

PIERRE walks about near her, combing his hair.

PIERRE: *That actor who was after you, have you seen him again?*

CHARLOTTE: *Why do you ask me that? You know very well that it's finished . . . that it didn't mean anything.*

PIERRE: *I ask you about it because I love you, Charlotte.*

He takes her by the waist.

CHARLOTTE annoyed: *Oh, please!*

PIERRE: *Why not?*

CHARLOTTE: *Not now.*

PIERRE: *Kiss me.*

We hear the leitmotif music and see CHARLOTTE's face in close-up. PIERRE's hand turns her face round and he kisses her. (*Still*) She turns away.

CHARLOTTE: *Anyway, you must know since you've had me followed by detectives.*

PIERRE: *That was only once, three months ago. You know that very well.*

CHARLOTTE: *Even if I had deceived you, you had no right.* He strokes her bare shoulder. *It proves that you didn't trust me.*

PIERRE: *Yes, it's true . . . you're right.*

He kisses her eye.

ROGER LEENHARDT now comes into the entrance hall of the block of flats. He pauses to look at the fresco signed ' Jean Cocteau 1962 '.

In the flat, NICHOLAS is in his bed, reading a child's illustrated paper. PIERRE's hand is seen, before he bends over to embrace his son.

PIERRE: *Goodnight, Nicholas.*

NICHOLAS putting aside his paper: *Oh, Daddy. You know, when I'm big, I shall go to Australia, to America . . . to England.*

PIERRE: *You're quite right.*

NICHOLAS: *To Scotland.*

PIERRE: *Go on, go to sleep.*

As he goes away, NICHOLAS picks up his paper again. CHARLOTTE comes in and kisses him.

CHARLOTTE: *Goodnight, Nicholas.*

NICHOLAS: *Goodnight. Where are you going this evening?*

CHARLOTTE: *We're going to stay and have dinner here, with the gentleman. And after that, we'll go to bed.* A pause. *Sleep well.*

NICHOLAS: *I will.*

CHARLOTTE: *Goodnight.*

NICHOLAS: *Goodnight.*

He picks up his paper again.

CHARLOTTE, still wearing her slip, is in the bathroom, reading a woman's magazine out loud. Opposite is a large wall mirror. We can hear NICHOLAS singing to himself.

CHARLOTTE: *'How to have a fashionable bust. Measure yourself with a tape-measure and compare the results with the ideal of a beautiful bust. There is an ideal bust-measurement. . . .* She gets up, still reading . . . *Compare the ideal figure, that of the Venus de Milo . . .'*

She puts the magazine on the washbasin, opened at the pages she was reading, and measures herself as the article indicates. (*Still*)

CHARLOTTE still reading aloud: *'. . . from the nipple in a horizontal line passing a centimeter below the middle of your arm. Hold the tape-measure straight, from your armpit to the hollow of your elbow. From your armpit . . .'* She does this. *' Take off a centimeter, divide in two . . . this is what your breast-measurement should be, according to your height.'*

PIERRE off: *Madame Céline . . . go and get us some leeks.*

MADAME CÉLINE: *But I wanted to go to the cinema.*

CHARLOTTE still following instructions in front of the mirror: *' You measure the distance from the base of your neck to the tip of your right breast . . .'* Looking at her tape-measure . . . *That ought to be twenty centimeters . . .* Reading again. *' You trace a secondary imaginary line from the base of your neck to the tip of your left breast . . .'* She ponders. *An imaginary line . . . twenty centimeters . . .* Reading again. *' You measure the distance between the tips of your two breasts.'* She does so. *Twenty centimeters.* Reading again. '*And these three measurements ought to form an equilateral triangle.*'

At these words, she stops, reflects, then shouts so that she can be heard in the next room.

CHARLOTTE: *Pierre, what does ' equilateral' mean?*

He comes into the bathroom towards her, a dress on each arm.

PIERRE: *Oh! I don't know.* He shows her the dresses. *Brown or green?*

CHARLOTTE: *The green.*

PIERRE: *I'll put it in the bedroom.*

CHARLOTTE: *Okay.*

We follow PIERRE as he goes out, then comes back holding an electric razor.

PIERRE: *I told you not to use my Phillips. Of course you've used it to shave your legs and thighs . . .*

CHARLOTTE off: *It wasn't me . . . it was Nicholas playing with it.*

We hear the child shouting:

NICHOLAS: *It's not true! It was Mummy! It was Mummy!*

CHARLOTTE puts on her dress.

PIERRE: *You see, you're lying!*

They are almost face-to-face, as he confronts her.

CHARLOTTE: *Why should I tell lies? It's a nasty thing to do.*

PIERRE: *But you do, sometimes, and so I've become suspicious.*

CHARLOTTE: *You've no right to say that!*

PIERRE: *You know very well what I'm talking about.*

CHARLOTTE: *It doesn't seem as though you have forgiven me.*

He slaps her.

PIERRE desolate: *It wasn't very hard. Anyway, I owed you a slap.*

She slaps him.

CHARLOTTE: *Not at all. I was a slap ahead. Now we're back to scratch again.*

He sits down and draws her towards him.

PIERRE: *Come here.*

CHARLOTTE: *No.*

PIERRE: *I won't hurt you.*

We see CHARLOTTE's face in close-up as he caresses it.

CHARLOTTE: *Look, we mustn't stop. He's waiting for us.*

PIERRE off: *Where do you begin? And where does the image I have of you end?* A pause. *In other words, how do I distinguish between the reality and the desire I have for it?*

CHARLOTTE: *You need only know what is behind my eyes.*

PIERRE off: *What is behind your eyes?*

CHARLOTTE: *Each time you come back from a trip, you ask me complicated questions.*

PIERRE off: *But I love you . . . and perhaps it's that . . . love itself is complicated.*

CHARLOTTE: *I love you too, Pierre . . . often it is not in the way you think, but it's sincere. Come on, we've got to go.*

In the living-room, PIERRE is sitting on a couch and lighting a cigar.

LEENHARDT off: *I didn't imagine your flat would be like this . . . it's unexpected, this setting, only twenty minutes from Paris.*

PIERRE: *Oh, places do exist which have not yet been touched by our time. Living away from the noise of the capital is a dream!*

As he stands up, we see the rest of the room. LEENHARDT sits in an armchair in the centre, and further off, CHARLOTTE is clearing away the dinner and laying out the cups for coffee.

CHARLOTTE: *Breathing in the rhythm of nature . . . as it was formed by past ages.*

As if to justify themselves, CHARLOTTE and PIERRE begin to recite what might be the house-agent's blurb for their flat.

Pan towards each of them as they take turns to speak.

CHARLOTTE: *Money cannot replace time when it comes to trees and plants.*

LEENHARDT partly off: *It's the 'escape' flat, an expression of the intent to build for man on the same scale as man.*

Now see them all. PIERRE is pouring a brandy, while CHARLOTTE is bustling about.

CHARLOTTE: *You will have noticed that the houses are spread around three parks which slope down gently towards the Seine, facing the magnificent forest of Marly.*

PIERRE talks as he walks around, brandy in hand.

PIERRE: *It's very well suited to human needs, is it not?*

CHARLOTTE comes into frame, carrying a tray of coffee.

CHARLOTTE: *We experience moments here, every day, which we would have thought otherwise to be exceptional . . .*

PIERRE: *Eight windows opening onto lawns and a walk in one's garden in the evening . . . that is really the life people were meant to live.*

CHARLOTTE sits down on the couch. PIERRE follows suit and kisses her tenderly.

CHARLOTTE: *Everything here is of the highest quality. From outside, you will have noticed the elegant façade of the building, which is a mixture of blocks of stone, mosaic and varnished mahogany.*

PIERRE: *Then I'll show you the bathroom. In it can be found not only thermostatically controlled mixer-taps, but also a dressing table where any woman would be happy to linger.*

CHARLOTTE: *One or two lumps of sugar?*

LEENHARDT: *None, please.*

PIERRE: *Have you seen my new television?*

LEENHARDT: *Ah! A Tele-Avia!*

PIERRE: *' The technique of aviation in the service of television.'*

While saying this, PIERRE has taken a model-aeroplane from the top of the T.V., and he plays with it. CHARLOTTE hands LEENHARDT his coffee. (*Still*)

PIERRE sitting down on the couch with the model plane in his hands: *Did you know that I flew from Düsseldorf to Rheims with the automatic pilot?*

CHARLOTTE: *The new one?*

PIERRE: *Yes.*

CHARLOTTE: *What's the use of having you there, if it's automatic?*

PIERRE: *In point of fact, it remembers better than I do.* CHARLOTTE sits down near him. *It's extraordinary, when you think about it, that the first thing one teaches a machine is to remember. To record the past!*

CHARLOTTE: *But the past isn't worth the trouble. The present is the important thing.*

TITLE white letters on black screen:

1   MEMORY

Close-up of PIERRE, chewing his cigar. As he speaks, he lights it, takes it out of his mouth, then replaces it between his lips.

PIERRE: *No, for me, memory is one of the most important things. But it's so incredible . . . for instance, when I was in Germany and*

I was at the Auschwitz trial for a few days, well, there were people there who were accused of having killed, oh, I don't know, thousands of people, and they didn't remember a thing. Well, perhaps that was because, oh, I don't know, perhaps it was a defence-mechanism, but really, with some of them one had the impression that they had just forgotten . . . and while we're talking about memory, you remember when I was in Italy with Monsieur Rossellini? Well, he told me a story. For him it was really the funniest story out. . . . A pause. Well, he told me that one day he was in the Champs-Elysées, and he saw a procession of people who had been deported . . . you know . . . they were still dressed as deportees, in their striped pyjamas. Ten years after. Well, naturally, they weren't still as thin as skeletons like when they came out of Dachau, or Mauthausen. They had eaten, they'd earned money since then. Close-up of CHARLOTTE, as she listens attentively. *Of course, they were living normally, they'd got fat.* Close-up of PIERRE, smoking. *It just didn't look right on them. Memory had got it all wrong, because they just didn't remember that they had changed. . . . Me, my memory, I can't help it. I would if I could, but I can't forget anything. I can remember my first flight as well as my holidays in Brittany. The first time I met you, do you remember? I can remember everything, even how I was dressed.* We hear a train in the distance, see CHARLOTTE's face in close-up as PIERRE concludes. *Of course, there are things which I would like to remember, but . . .*

TITLE white letters on black screen:

2 THE PRESENT

Close-up of CHARLOTTE, speaking.
CHARLOTTE: *Memory, all that, its unnecessary. I prefer the present. The present is more exciting.* Close-up of PIERRE. *I like music. . . . I like things that are perishable. . . . I like flowers, I like . . .*
PIERRE talking to himself: *That makes me think . . .*
Resume on CHARLOTTE.
CHARLOTTE: *Love. Love. You have to live it. Of course, you have to live in the present, because if there is no present, it's not living, it dies.* A pause. *The most important thing for me is to understand*

what is happening to me, to see what it resembles. . . . *Everything that I have known, that I have seen in others . . . it's difficult! It's difficult in the present. . . . That's why I like it, because, during the present I haven't got time to reflect, I can't think.* She glances at her husband. *What did you say? No, I can't understand . . . I can't understand, the present is stronger than I am. Of course, the thing I love, the thing that fascinates me, is the element that escapes me, that I can't control in the present. . . . And that's why I like it. I want to be able to control because I think. It's because I can't help myself from thinking, and because I'm not an animal. . . . Sometimes, I'm sorry I'm not. I like animals. They're so natural, their movements are so natural. Animals are always beautiful. But there we are, we are always forced to try and understand. Well, am I happy?* A pause. *No, I'm not happy because, well, precisely because I have no life in the present. Because I'm quite clear in myself, I'm not surprised by anything that happens to me.* A pause. *Yes, yes, there are lots of things I am ashamed of. Precisely because when they happened, I wasn't able to prepare myself. I didn't know. No, I was ashamed afterwards. I was ashamed because I hadn't been able to recognize that I shouldn't have done it.* She shakes her head. *But while it was happening, no. Not during the present. I can't, it escapes me. I don't know what is happening. The present stops one from going mad . . .*

TITLE white letters on black screen:

3 INTELLIGENCE

Close-up of LEENHARDT.

LEENHARDT: *It's curious how certain words, which didn't seem particularly important when one heard them, after a certain time take on an almost central significance. I'm thinking of something a friend said to me, twenty-five years ago, yes, it was in 1940 in the middle of the disaster, at Vichy. He was a very brave man, a clever man. He was one of the first to join the Resistance . . . but before definitively taking sides, he wanted to come to Vichy to see for himself. 'You see,' he told me, 'I'm a man who likes to understand before I affirm.' Well, this friend, who had a fine Christian name, Emmanuel, was not like me in the least . . . but his aphorism has* become a sort of personal motto to me, which I say as a joke, but which is, in my belief, the most serious definition which exists of intelligence. Intelligence is to understand before affirming. It means that when confronted with an idea, one seeks to go beyond it. . . . To find its limits, to find its opposite. . . . Consequently, it is to understand others. Gradually to seek out a little path between the ' for ' and the ' against ', between oneself and the others. Oh, I know that not everybody finds this morality of the intellect sympathetic. Especially not today, when people like primary colours and find it a bit grey to hunt for the nuances between black and white. But I must confess that it is the fanatics, the dogmatists who are really the boring ones, in my opinion. First of all, one always knows in advance what they are going to say, while on the other hand, people who are not so much sceptical as fond of paradoxes, are amusing, and the essence of the paradox is, in the face of what seems a per-fectly self-evident idea, to look for the opposite. And then, today, we also need the word ' compromise '. A pause. Compromise is one of the most beautiful, the most courageous of intellectual opera-tions. Compromise has become a perjorative word. It has come to mean compromising with one's principles. But for myself, I'm going to carry on. . . . CHARLOTTE in close-up . . . thinking that one has to seek for a proper synthesis. Resume on LEENHARDT in close-up. And I will continue to say that the world is not totally absurd. That it is precisely the role of intelligence to seek to what degree one can put a little bit of reason into this absurdity. Do you know, Madame, that despite your very light brown hair, you make me think of a beautiful redhead. ' La Jolie Rousse ' is a poem by Apollinaire. ' Soleil voici le temps de la raison ardente. . . .' Well, that burning-bright reason which the poet is looking for. . . . Resume on CHARLOTTE . . . when it does appear, it takes on the form of a beautiful redhead. That is what can be seen on a woman's face, the presence of awareness, something which gives her a different, an extra beauty. Resume on LEENHARDT in close-up. Feminine beauty becomes some-thing all-powerful, and it's for that reason, I believe, that all the great ideas in French are in the feminine gender . . . that there are statues called ' La Vertu ', ' La République ', ' La France '. . . . But I realize for my part that it is ridiculous to make this little speech on philosophy in the context of a social evening, but I do ask you to believe one thing. Firstly, that it is sincere, and secondly, that it *is not because I am growing old that I make this declaration of intellectual prudence. When I was twenty, in fact, I was even more open to others, and it's now, when one's sixty, that one wants to give one's intellect a holiday from time to time, that humanism becomes a heavy burden to bear and that one has the desire to do foolish things. . . . I don't know if I'll manage to do it, but in any case, I believe that we ought to love wise young people and mad old ones.*

TITLE white letters on black screen:

4   CHILDHOOD

A door opens and a half-asleep NICHOLAS comes into close-up.
NICHOLAS: *For the job. Firstly, you think about it, secondly, you make calculations, thirdly, you warn everybody. . . . Fourthly, you do it. . . . Fifthly, you buy the paint. . . . Sixthly, you check everything. . . . Seventhly, you paint it. . . . Eighthly, you re-check everything. . . . Ninthly, you add the finishing touches. . . . Tenthly, you set it in motion.*

In the bedroom, we see a record sleeve in close-up: EROTIC, THE RHYTHMS OF LOVE. CHARLOTTE's hand lifts it to reveal another, WOMEN: FRANK POURCEL AND HIS FRENCH STRINGS, (*Still*) then another, BELLY DANCE FOR YOUR HUSBAND, and two others in the same style.
CHARLOTTE off: *What are these records?*
PIERRE off: *A chap in West Berlin gave me them for one of his friends in N.A.T.O. here.*
We see the room. CHARLOTTE is sitting on the bed in her nightdress, looking at the records.
CHARLOTTE: *Oh, I'd like to hear that one.*
PIERRE comes up behind her in his pyjamas.
PIERRE: *No, don't, they're not ours.*
She gets up and walks through into the living-room. We look across the two rooms from the outside balcony.
PIERRE off: *Charlotte. No!*
She puts the EROTIC record on the gramophone.
CHARLOTTE: *Listen . . . it doesn't hurt them. Do listen!*

Hysterical female laughter is heard on the record. PIERRE approaches. Cut to a little later, the same sound. He is standing in the background, lighting a cigarette, while she sits beside the half-cleared table. Irritated by the persistent laughter, she stands up. He listens, agitated, but with an impassive face.

CHARLOTTE: *I'm thirsty.*

She goes out, passing in front of him, then comes back and pours herself a glass of water. PIERRE sits down and plays with his model aeroplane. She walks about in front of him for a moment, then she goes towards the bedroom.

CHARLOTTE: *I want to put on another.*

PIERRE: *No, that's enough.*

CHARLOTTE: *I want to.*

PIERRE getting up quickly: *I told you, they aren't ours.*

He chases her and catches her as she comes out of the bedroom at the same time as him. He seizes her wrist.

PIERRE: *Put that record down . . . or I'll rape you.*

CHARLOTTE struggling out of his grasp: *Stop that! You're out of your mind!*

PIERRE: *No, you're very beautiful.*

CHARLOTTE: *No, no, you're going to have a run for your money.*

PIERRE starts chasing her again through the two rooms.

PIERRE pursuing her: *I told you they were not ours!*

As the chase continues, we see rapid close-ups of record sleeves: first, the face of Marlene Dietrich, then, a portrait of Beethoven. As she goes by the gramophone, CHARLOTTE manages to put the record on, but PIERRE finally catches her.

CHARLOTTE off, referring to the Beethoven record: *Who's that?*

PIERRE off: *That? I don't know. Old music.*

We look down on the gramophone as CHARLOTTE's hand puts on the record.

CHARLOTTE: *Can I put it on?*

The music starts, a Beethoven quartet.

PIERRE off: *Yes . . . if you're nice.*

CHARLOTTE off: *I will be.*

Close-up of her shoulder as PIERRE slides down the strap of her nightdress. They kiss each other on the lips. Now, we look down on the sheet: two hands wearing wedding rings grasp each other. We see PIERRE's profile, kissing her forehead repeatedly. His lips frame an unheard 'I love you' with each kiss. As the commentary begins, we see a close-up of the words HIGH FIDELITY, then pan to the bottom half of a magazine on which we see the words NOUS CON- before the camera moves on to CERNE. An article about the film *Jules & Jim* is just visible above these words.

COMMENTARY off: *You know I don't like that. Did you miss me? I'm sorry in darkness. Why? Gently. It's too complicated. I'm afraid. My love.*

We see four hands washing each other in the wash-basin.

COMMENTARY off: *I am sad. The water is cold. I shut my eyes. Because. . . . Yes, I remember it. Always like that. He looked into my eyes.*

Close-up of the couple, with their arms wrapped round each other. PIERRE unhooks her bra, his hands caress her back, while CHARLOTTE strokes her own hair. We see her in close-up, wearing her pyjamas, as they kiss each other.

Another shot of her face as PIERRE strokes her cheek, while she lies back on the pillow. She kisses his finger. We look down on her legs, first lying, then standing on the bed as he kisses her knees. Close-up of CHARLOTTE's face, lying down.

COMMENTARY off: *Besides, it's not your fault. There is one little thing. I bought myself a new dress. He doesn't talk. A week afterwards. When we are dead. With lassitude. Our legs and my thighs. It doesn't matter. All these awful scenes. Don't be like that.*

We see four bare legs get out of a bath, which are then covered by a towel.

Now the legs are interlaced on the bed, seen from above.
Cut quickly to her navel, then to the back of PIERRE's neck, as he kisses her lying under him.

COMMENTARY off: *I have loved you. Weakness. Truth. I want to know. I'll explain to you. He left quickly.*

We see CHARLOTTE's legs, standing on the bed while he kisses her calf, then we cut to her head, thrown back.

COMMENTARY: *On the contrary. There. I promise you that that's how it is. Once again. Like before. To regret. On that evening. On that evening. Nothing had ever . . . love.*

Dissolve to her legs, raised from the bed.

CHARLOTTE singing off:

> ' *Of infinite sadness*
> *Love is like the day*
> *It goes away . . . goes away*
> *Love is like the day . . .'*

PIERRE's hands caress her legs, while she is singing.

CHARLOTTE off:

> ' *Of infinite tenderness*
> *Love is like the day*
> *It comes back . . . it comes back*
> *Love is like the day . . .'*

We look down on her bare legs and PIERRE's head as he kisses her knees. (*Still*)

CHARLOTTE off: *Are we going on holiday this year?*

PIERRE: *That depends. I don't know yet. Did I tell you that last Tuesday I met the chap who had met you at the Club Méditerranée?*

CHARLOTTE off: *A Canadian?*

PIERRE: *Yes.*

CHARLOTTE: *Yes, he was a creep.*

PIERRE: *He was after you.*

CHARLOTTE off: *You knew that when I met you, you were the second, not the first.* A pause. *You seem upset.*

PIERRE off: *No, no, that's all right.*

CHARLOTTE off: *It's odd, but men will allow something for themselves which they will not allow for women.*

We see CHARLOTTE's profile as she sits on the bed, facing PIERRE.

CHARLOTTE: *It was a silly thing to do, to rape me, and slap me. It's not the way to make me be nice to you.*

PIERRE: *I'm sorry.*

CHARLOTTE: *Oh, you're always saying that, but you don't really ever forgive yourself.*

PIERRE: *I do sometimes.*

CHARLOTTE: *You can go fast in your plane . . . emotions aren't like that.*

PIERRE: *I agree.*

They kiss. Now we see CHARLOTTE from behind PIERRE's neck, as she puts her arms round it and strokes his hair.

CHARLOTTE: *If I asked you what your faults were, what would you say?*

PIERRE: *Why? I'd rather tell you about my qualities . . .*

CHARLOTTE: *No, it's your faults that I'm interested in.*

PIERRE: *Pride, impatience, my love for you . . .*

CHARLOTTE: *For me, it's laziness, untruthfulness, no, not so much laziness. . . . But I haven't any will-power.*

> CHARLOTTE, wearing her night-dress, has her back to us, as PIERRE's hand comes into frame.

PIERRE off: *Take off your nightie.*

CHARLOTTE: *No, I'll be cold.*

PIERRE off, withdrawing his hand: *You said that you would be nice.*
> She takes off her night-dress, revealing her bare back, which he begins to stroke.

PIERRE off: *Why don't you like looking at me any more?*

CHARLOTTE: *What exactly does that mean?*

> PIERRE kisses her shoulder, then he goes out of frame.

PIERRE: *Re-garder, I don't know if that means ' garder deux fois '.*

CHARLOTTE: *If it means keeping something twice, then it's precious!*
> Music, as we dissolve to her face, with one of PIERRE's fingers stroking under her chin.

PIERRE off: *Yes. You're sad, suddenly.*

CHARLOTTE: *Yes.*

PIERRE off: *Because of me?*

CHARLOTTE: *No. Because of people.*

PIERRE off: *What do you mean?*

CHARLOTTE: *I don't know. Everybody. All the people in the street. . . . I'd like to know. . . . I'd like to get to know them all . . . that one, that one, that one. This one may be going to die tomorrow. He's waiting for a telephone call before killing himself. It doesn't come, and so he kills himself! We are all guilty!*

PIERRE off: *I'll always be here.*

> His hand slides over the sheet; CHARLOTTE grasps it.

CHARLOTTE off: *What film was it in? There was a sailor and a little girl. . . . He took her in his arms and he went round and round with her, and it was done very slowly?*

PIERRE off: *Oh yes, in slow motion . . .*

CHARLOTTE: *I don't know. It was beautiful. How do they do that?*

PIERRE off: *I don't know. Cinema is a mystery.*

Close-up of PIERRE, wearing only his pyjama trousers. CHARLOTTE's hand strokes him, moving up from his stomach to his chest.

PIERRE off: *When are we going to have a child?*

CHARLOTTE off: *You've already got one.*

PIERRE off: *But I'd like to have a child by you.*

CHARLOTTE off: *Have you been thinking about it for a long time?*

PIERRE off: *Ever since I've known you.*

Close-up of PIERRE's face, as the leitmotiv music begins.

CHARLOTTE off: *I'm happy! I'm happy! I'm happy! I'm happy! I'm happy! I'm happy! I'm hap . . . happy.*

We look down on CHARLOTTE's head as she lies, asleep. The telephone rings. A pause, before we see her move to pick it up and lie back in the pillows, holding the receiver.

CHARLOTTE into telephone: *I said you weren't to telephone me at home. A pause. At Marseilles! What are you going to do at Marseilles? A pause. ' Berenice.' A pause. There is no cinema at Orly. What? A pause. All right. Okay, quarter past four, five o'clock at the cinema at Orly. A pause. Seat No. 12. Okay. A pause. I'll blow you a kiss, too.*

She replaces the receiver. Looking more serious, she dials another number. We move away from her as a telephone rings off. She listens and replies.

CHARLOTTE into telephone: *Hello, is that Doctor Deotot? Good morning, Doctor, this is Madame Giraud speaking. Er, I wanted to ask you . . . could I come at half-past three instead of three o'clock because I'm working today and I don't think I shall have finished by three. . . . Good, thank you! Have you got the results? . . . Thank you, Doctor. I'll see you this afternoon.*

She puts back the receiver and lies back on her pillow for a moment, murmuring:

CHARLOTTE: *Not to be . . .!*

She sighs. Sounds can be heard of work outside.

CHARLOTTE is now in her bath. The din of the work outside is intercut by the ringing of a telephone.

MADAME CÉLINE shouting off: *It's for you!*

We see CHARLOTTE's bare legs getting out of the bath.

CHARLOTTE off: *Tell them I've already gone out.*

MADAME CÉLINE off: *It's your husband.*

We see CHARLOTTE's legs as she dries herself.

CHARLOTTE off: *What does he want?*

MADAME CÉLINE off: *He says he's waking you up as he promised, and he asks if you're going to have lunch with him? He says it won't be easy, because he's only got half an hour.*

CHARLOTTE off: *Right . . . well, tell him that I'll come and fetch him this evening, and send him a kiss from me.*

Her hand comes down to her legs to cut off the hairs on them, then we come close to her face as she cuts strands of hair from her head, then we go to her hand, holding a small pair of scissors, moving down her body. Dissolve to her fully dressed, as she goes out of the bedroom, and along the balcony into the living-room, where the maid is sitting, reading a woman's magazine.

MADAME CÉLINE: *Madame, what does ' equilateral ' mean?*

CHARLOTTE: *Raymonde, how many times have I told you not to touch my papers and my things?*

The maid puts down the paper and goes to pick up the vacuum-cleaner.

MADAME CÉLINE: *And how many times have I told you to call me Madame Céline, and not by my Christian name?*

CHARLOTTE goes out onto the balcony. Facing the block of flats is an enormous work-yard with numerous cranes. We hear a confusion of noises.

CHARLOTTE: *If Madame Leroy telephones, tell her that I'm going straight to the swimming pool. I won't go to the office.*

The camera pans over the wall of the block of flats to the kitchen-window. As the maid clears away the remains of the meal, she drinks enthusiastically the remains of a bottle of wine.

MADAME CÉLINE: *Well, what does ' equilateral ' mean?*

The two women stand at the sink, facing the window. CHARLOTTE is drinking.

CHARLOTTE: *Why, are you interested? But you have such a nice bust!*

MADAME CÉLINE: *Oh. . . . It's thanks to Peruvian Serum.*

CHARLOTTE: *What's that?*

MADAME CÉLINE: *Just a moment. I'll show you.* As she goes out, there is an explosion in the workyard. She comes back, thumbing through a paper. *There!*

She walks up and down the room, reading out the vital item.
CHARLOTTE follows her attentively.

MADAME CÉLINE: *Exclusive. How to double the size of your breasts.*
The answer is Peruvian Serum. The secret of beautiful breasts is
revealed. By whom? Peruvian doctors were the originators of this
fabulous discovery. Thanks to Peruvian Serum, you will notice a
rapid improvement, whatever the shape of your breasts, whatever
your age, in size and form. Give your husband a delightful surprise.

She bursts out laughing.

TITLE white letters on black screen:

5   THE JAVA

The maid is washing the dishes. Cut to CHARLOTTE sitting in
the middle of the room, facing her.

CHARLOTTE: *Was* your *husband pleased?*

(The Java is the name of a French popular dance. The following speech was cut at the last stage of editing. Like the second
long speech, which does appear in the film, it was adapted from
Céline's *Death on the Instalment Plan*.)

[MADAME CÉLINE: *I'll say he was. At the beginning, he wasn't*
interested. He dragged about like a wet dish-rag. His trousers were
hanging in great bags around his knees, like an elephant's hide. He
hardly said hello to me when I came back from doing my cleaning
. . . he was going downhill. But now it's quite a different story.
Madame. He's never seen his Raymonde in her pink satin before.
Oh! Yes! Beautiful breasts! And did I wiggle my hips! I undulated.
It's my gorgeous tits that did it. Worked like a charm. He didn't
know what had hit him. He trembled, he shook all over, he clenched
his fists, he rocked the stool he was sitting on till it creaked. He
comes and puffs a mixture of insults and sweet things up my
nose. . . . I get all stirred up . . . so hot! He goes head over heels
like a ninepin. Then he grabs me and pins me to the ground, and
bundles over on top of me. I dig my fingers into his fat neck. He
starts to bellow . . . that's done it! I'm on my knees straddling him,
I've got my two hands full . . . squeezing, pulling. I just keep my
arse fixed on him. He flails about, the great brute, he's almost at

the end of his tether. I'm all burning, my breasts are on fire. We're stuck, we can't move, then all at once he's recovered . . . and this time it's me that exhausted. Bugger it! If only I'd had just a second more. . . . I haven't yet taken the littlest . . . the littlest. . . . Oh, I'm finished. My eyelids shut like a clamp. What a bout! Oh yes, the blokes want to have it all night . . . they shout, they bawl . . . the dirty brutes. He's so fat! So then I lie under him. I'm in my favourite position. Background music, the very rhythmic, ' Le Jazz et la Java '. He sweeps me down like a whirlwind, and I feel a shock running through my whole body. I want to get free. I arch, I buck, I crawl about the remains of myself. My tits are pulverised. I can't find a place to breathe. I collapse under his kisses . . . my breasts . . . spasms. . . . I push my tongue down his throat to stop him crying out. I push my fingers in any hole I can. I use all my energy, I use all my skill, but he's got me just the same. So I let myself go, he goes wild. His great swollen hands grab my arse from behind. I want to anchor him so that he just stops moving. There! It's over. It's marvellous, it's fucking, fucking marvellous. I'm just one solid mass of beauty. I'm my whole self all joined together at last in beauty. . . . Oh, love! The only true joy in the world! The only deliverance, the only truth! . . . Oh, harmony! To find harmony! To find harmony!

TITLE read from right to left so that the last word is visible first:

DEATH ON THE INSTALLMENT PLAN]

In the entrance hall to the block of flats, CHARLOTTE passes the Cocteau fresco and goes out.

COMMENTARY off: *Like at the cinema. The sky is blue. Abolish the past. Put on lipstick. What are you thinking about? I'm hesitating. The day after. He didn't know.*

At the swimming-bath, the commentary continues. Large letters appear on the screen, gradually reading AMERI . . . followed by various shots in negative of models in bathing suits, posing, playing in the pool, swimming, diving, playing.

COMMENTARY off: *In the clouds, get undressed. If I were you, I wouldn't go. The evening of the day after. Tuesday afternoon. Very rapidly. For several days, in January 1964. And anyway, I think its fun. It's nerves. Freed from that hope. Nothing had changed. One last time. The new apartment. The telephone rings. It's lovely weather. Not to him, not to anyone. Why should I? We will go where you like. It had stopped raining. We heard nothing. One must choose.*

A photographer faces camera. He loads his camera, puts it to his eye and takes some shots. We see these in the negative and then, as the commentary ends, CHARLOTTE, also in negative with her hair and eyes and lips in brilliant white, comes into the vestibule which leads to the swimming-bath.

COMMENTARY off: *At first I said nothing. What is the matter? Tenderness of course, all imaginable suffering. A face bathed in tears. Stroking my hair. I remained silent. To look around one.*

We hear swimming-bath noises as the picture returns to normal.

Some models in swimsuits come into frame. The camera pans towards CHARLOTTE, walking and talking with a COLLEAGUE on the magazine for which she works.

COLLEAGUE to CHARLOTTE: *It's finished.*

Another negative shot as CHARLOTTE passes the PHOTOGRAPHER.

CHARLOTTE to the PHOTOGRAPHER: *Will you drop me at the Trocadero?*

PHOTOGRAPHER: *Yes, but I must make some telephone calls first.*

CHARLOTTE: *Okay, I'll wait for you in the bar.*

Normal picture again as she picks up her handbag, quickly kisses her colleague, and goes off.

At the swimming-bath bar, CHARLOTTE is sitting at a table. Behind her, we see the Seine through a bay window.

VOICE off, reading: *A girl, the sun, Uranus and Saturn will help you to come to decisions about very important projects. Be careful of somebody who may feel that they have been defeated or betrayed, and may be jealous. Adopt a passive attitude. The situation is complicated and uncertain. It is vital that you overcome your anxiety or your dissatisfaction. Do not let yourself give way to discouragement or depression . . .*

CHARLOTTE turning towards the voice: *Will you lend it to me?*

A hand gives her the magazine.

CHARLOTTE: *Thank you.*

We see the cover of Elle magazine, a close-up of a model's face.

FIRST GIRL off: *Have you seen this girl with a topless?*

SECOND GIRL off: *What's that?*

Close-up of CHARLOTTE's profile, as she starts to flip through the magazine.

FIRST GIRL off: *You know, those swimming suits with no top, just braces. . . . Look!*

SECOND GIRL off: *Oh no! She must be going hot and cold all over.*

FIRST GIRL off: *No. . . . I think they're nice. Wouldn't you like to wear one?*

SECOND GIRL off: *No. . . . Never!*

During this exchange, we have been looking down at the advertisements in CHARLOTTE's magazine, mostly ones for bras and girdles. In the background there is the usual noise of a bar, the hum of conversation, the sound of bar-billiards.

FIRST GIRL off: *But look, if that does come into fashion, I don't see why one shouldn't wear it . . . then you've seen how they make that, too. Yes, because I know they also put flowers on the navel.*

SECOND GIRL off: *No top, just on the navel?*

FIRST GIRL off: *Yes, I've seen it. And have you seen now, instead of wearing a bra, they just put a scarf round their neck, as if, er, as if it were the top of a swim suit. Super! Don't you think so?*

SECOND GIRL off: *Oh no . . .*

CHARLOTTE looks down at an advertisement for panties.

FIRST GIRL off: *I don't know, but you'll see! I'm sure that in a few years everybody will be wearing them.*

SECOND GIRL off: *No. I don't think it's decent, really.*

FIRST GIRL off: *I know.*

SECOND GIRL off: *When are you going on your holidays?*

Close-ups of the advertisement in CHARLOTTE's magazine.

FIRST GIRL off: *At the end of the month . . . er. . . . Yes, certainly.*

SECOND GIRL off: *Where are you going?*

FIRST GIRL off: *To Majorca.*

SECOND GIRL off: *Who with?*

FIRST GIRL off: *My parents can't go with me this year, so they've given me my freedom. I can go alone. But actually, I'm going with Patrick.*

SECOND GIRL off: *With Patrick?*

FIRST GIRL off: *Yes, we're going by car if he has one. He's done his baccalaureat, so he should be getting a car . .*

SECOND GIRL off: *I'm going with my parents. Well, parents are all right, but you can't go out in the evening.*

FIRST GIRL off: *I'll have my freedom. I'll be out every night.*

CHARLOTTE is flipping through her magazine without looking at it. Her face is thoughtful as she listens to the two girls talking. We can see them now in the background, their backs towards us, sitting at a nearby table.

SECOND GIRL: *But I do go out during the day, until ten o'clock at night.*

FIRST GIRL: *But it's after ten o'clock that you have all the fun. That's holidays.*

SECOND GIRL: *But a boy is too much to put up with day and night.*

FIRST GIRL: *There's a party at Rouch's this evening. Would you like to come?*

SECOND GIRL: *Thank you, but I can't. I have to go to a friend's.*

FIRST GIRL: *Are you going to the cinema?*

SECOND GIRL: *No, I've got to go to his house.*

FIRST GIRL: *Are you going to do the baccalaureat next year?*

SECOND GIRL: *Oh yes, sure!*

FIRST GIRL: *Which school do you go to?*

SECOND GIRL: *Pontoise. Where do you go?*

FIRST GIRL: *The Molière.*

TITLE moving slowly across the screen, letter by letter:

WHAT EVERY WOMAN SHOULD KNOW

Resume on CHARLOTTE's face.

TITLE moving slowly across the screen, letter by letter:

SHE KNOWS IT

Close-up of SECOND GIRL, drinking through a straw.

Close-up of FIRST GIRL.

TITLE moving slowly across the screen, letter by letter:

SHE DOESN'T KNOW

CHARLOTTE's face is still thoughtful.

Now we see the bar from the table of the two girls. In the background, CHARLOTTE has her back to us, but her face is slightly turned to listen to their conversation, which for us is drowned by the noise of the bar, especially the bar-billiards. (*Still*)

Across CHARLOTTE's back and between the two girls, the conversation is summarized in sub-titles:

SUB-TITLES: *I sleep with a boy. I don't know what to do. He will caress you. Switch out the light. I shall have to undress! He will be naked! In the darkness. No time. To stop thinking. Atmosphere. Always afraid. He will see my breasts . . .*

Close-up of CHARLOTTE as she turns towards them. A Sylvie Vartan pop-song begins on the juke-box.

The song continues as we see a magazine advertisement for men's bathing trunks, panning over it from top to bottom, then from left to right. Then a new insert: BE ATTRACTIVE, before we move across to a photo of a bra. More advertisements in the same style follow, then part of a comic-strip. It shows a vamp surrounded by men, with the words: I KNOW, BUT THIS EVENING I WANT TO BELIEVE IN MY ILLUSIONS, AND FORGET ALL ABOUT DETAILS OF THIS SINISTER AFFAIR. Two more advertisements for lipstick and Kotex are followed by this announcement:

DON'T BE JEALOUS. YOU TOO CAN HAVE THE YOUNG MODERN DYNAMIC FIGURE WHICH YOU ENVY IN OTHER WOMEN. WEAR ELOQUENCE, THE NEW BRA-CREATION BY JEUNESSE.

We are shown a girdle, a bra, a model's face, a succession of feminine-angled advertisements.

CHARLOTTE's head can be seen at the bottom of the screen, as she walks past a giant boarding showing a woman in a bra. (*Still*) She pauses between the two breasts.

In another street, we are at ground-level near a newspaper kiosk. CHARLOTTE's feet pass in front of a newspaper advertisement, on which we can see the words: FRANCE DIMANCHE, and also in large letters: HOW FAR CAN A WOMAN GO IN LOVE? Next to it, a photograph of General de Gaulle, dating from the period of June 18th, looks out from a copy of *La Voix de la France*. As CHARLOTTE's legs go round the kiosk, we move back to the word HOW in the first advertisement.

A door opens and CHARLOTTE comes in. She is led by the RECEPTIONIST to the door of the doctor's surgery.

RECEPTIONIST: *The doctor is coming.*

CHARLOTTE: *Thank you.*

In the surgery, CHARLOTTE goes towards the desk, sits down, then gets up to take a book from the desk. As she sits down and thumbs through an anatomy of gynaecology, we look down on the pages which can be lifted up to show different views of internal organs. We hear the door.

THE DOCTOR off: *Good-day, Madame.*

CHARLOTTE off: *Good-day, Doctor.* A pause. *Well?*

DOCTOR off: *Your fears are now confirmed. The results of the laboratory tests are positive. You are three months pregnant. You will probably have your baby in May.*

CHARLOTTE off: *Oh.*

She shuts the book and we look down on her hands, folded over it.

DOCTOR off: *You don't seem completely delighted about this happy event.*

We come close to CHARLOTTE as she says:

CHARLOTTE: *Doctor, I'm worried. I'm frightened by the idea. Can you give me painless childbirth?*

DOCTOR off: *Well, painless childbirth is just a manner of speaking.*

TITLE white letters on black screen:

6   PLEASURE AND SCIENCE

We see first the DOCTOR's face in close-up, then CHARLOTTE, rubbing her cheeks, as he explains.

DOCTOR: *What we mean by painless childbirth is preparing the mother-to-be psychologically for this important event which is, unfortunately, only too often distorted in popular belief by gruesome old-wives' tales.*

Close-up of the DOCTOR again.

CHARLOTTE off: *Doctor, there is one question that I have always wanted to ask you. What do you think about methods of contraception?*

DOCTOR embarrassed: *Well, that is a most important question, most important.* He smiles. *One which is receiving a lot of attention at present. It is a most obvious fact that in an age when we are at the point of sending rockets to the moon, we still conceive, on the surface of this earth, as our ancestors did in the Stone Age. Er, quite often it is under the worst, the most unsuitable conditions, the most contrary to nature. In our dealings with animals and plants, we are, thanks to scientific developments, now going about things in a different way, selecting the finest specimens of animal and plant species for the purpose of reproduction, and putting them in the most appropriate conditions, in order to obtain the best possible results.*

Close-up of CHARLOTTE.

DOCTOR off: *But so far as the human race is concerned, we are doing the exact opposite: consequently, it is going to be necessary, sooner or later, to control and direct conception.*

Resume on the DOCTOR.

CHARLOTTE off: *I have a problem. I'm hesitating between two men and, now that I'm pregnant, I don't know which of them is the father. Is physical pleasure a proof?*

DOCTOR: *I really can't go along with you there. We are occasionally obliged to operate in certain ways, for instance artificial insemination. In such a case, physical pleasure doesn't enter into it, since the patient simply undergoes a surgical operation.*

CHARLOTTE off: *But . . . but . . . pleasure . . . and . . . love. . . . Is that the same thing?*

DOCTOR: *Pleasure and love are phys . . . two different things. . . . Pleasure . . .*

CHARLOTTE off: *Is physical pleasure wrong?*

DOCTOR: *No, it's not wrong, since it normally results in the desired event of conception.*

CHARLOTTE off: *I'm frightened.*

At a crossroad in Paris, we follow CHARLOTTE through the street, as people pass her or cross the road. She walks past an enormous boarding. A workman on a stepladder is covering it with an advertisement for a certain make of bra. She runs across the road, slips, and falls on the pavement. She gets up quickly.

TITLE:

EVE
REVES

We hear the music as, in another part of Paris, CHARLOTTE runs towards a taxi, looks right and left, then gets in.

TITLE:

WHAT WILL BE

The taxi stops. CHARLOTTE gets out quickly, pays, walks a few yards, hails another taxi and gets in.

Inside the taxi, CHARLOTTE, wearing dark glasses, crouches against the seat and looks out of the back window.

We move with the taxi as it goes through the tunnel leading to the southern motorway which passes Orly. At the turning, we move out to a winking DANGER sign.

Outside the airport, the taxi stops by one of the glass entrance doors. We hear the flight announcements being made as CHARLOTTE gets out of the taxi.

Now we are on the ground floor of the airport, looking up at a rotating chandelier in the form of a globe. The usual airport noises can be heard, as we come close to CHARLOTTE. Still wearing her dark glasses, she is leaning against a wall by the place for admission tickets to the various flight levels. She looks around to make sure she is not being followed. We see a large neon sign reading: HOTEL-CINEMA, then return to CHARLOTTE as she walks towards the escalators. Her hand is placed on the rail of the escalator, going up. We see her legs, motionless on the step, then the emergency button and the words: EMERGENCY STOP. The screen lightens, as the escalator rises towards the huge bay-window on the first floor. We move with CHARLOTTE, past one of the bars and the shop-windows, towards the cinema. We see an advertisement for Hitchcock's *Spellbound*, but CHARLOTTE hurries past the box-office without looking at it.

CHARLOTTE to the woman in the box-office: *One please. Thank you.* We watch her go to the entrance of the auditorium. She has second thoughts, takes off her glasses and goes to look at the illuminated seat-plan. She chooses her seat by pressing a button and goes in. A quick close-up of a portrait of Alfred Hitchcock. In the auditorium, we look from the screen at the seats. ROBERT is sitting in the middle of a row at the back. Near to us, there is another spectator. He turns towards CHARLOTTE and smiles, as she comes in and sits down two rows away from ROBERT. When she has got accustomed to the darkness, CHARLOTTE scans the auditorium, gets up and goes to sit next to ROBERT. Neither of them speak. We see the screen as the curtains are withdrawn. Music begins as we look back at ROBERT and CHARLOTTE, who face us, watching the screen. Alain Resnais' *Night and Fog* is being shown, and we hear the sound of its commentary.

THE SPEAKER off: *Even a peaceful countryside, even a meadow with flights of crows, harvests and bonfires . . .*

CHARLOTTE puts her hand on ROBERT's knees. On the screen, we see a plot of land surrounded by barbed wire. CHARLOTTE in close-up turns her head towards ROBERT. We see his profile, looking at the screen.

THE SPEAKER off: *. . . Even a road with cars, peasants, couples going along it. . . .* On the screen, a barely-furnished room is shown, then a landscape. . . . *Even a holiday village with a fair, and a steeple, can lead to a concentration camp.*

ROBERT's eyes are on the screen. Finally, both he and CHARLOTTE turn away.

THE SPEAKER off: *Stuthof, Oranienburg, Auschwitz, Neuengamme, Belsen, Ravensbruck, Dachau, were all names like any others on the maps and in the guide-books . . .*

ROBERT and CHARLOTTE get up and go out.

On the first floor of the air-terminal, we look at the illuminated seat-plan: two of the seat-buttons go out. We follow ROBERT and CHARLOTTE as they walk across the hall, a long way apart. CHARLOTTE glances to left and right; behind her is ROBERT, carrying a small suitcase. He goes towards the hotel. She sits down behind a pillar near the hotel. He comes back without his suitcase, passes by her, and drops a key. She bends to pick

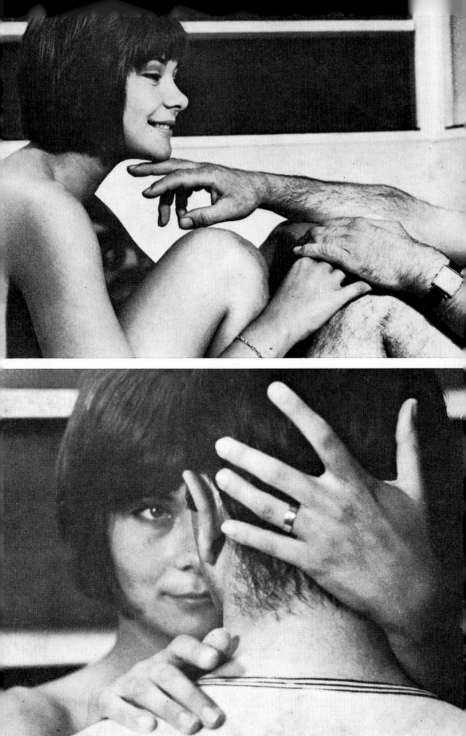

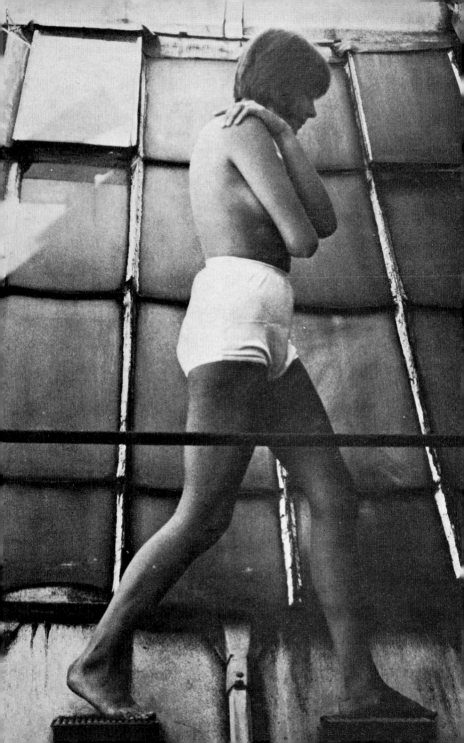

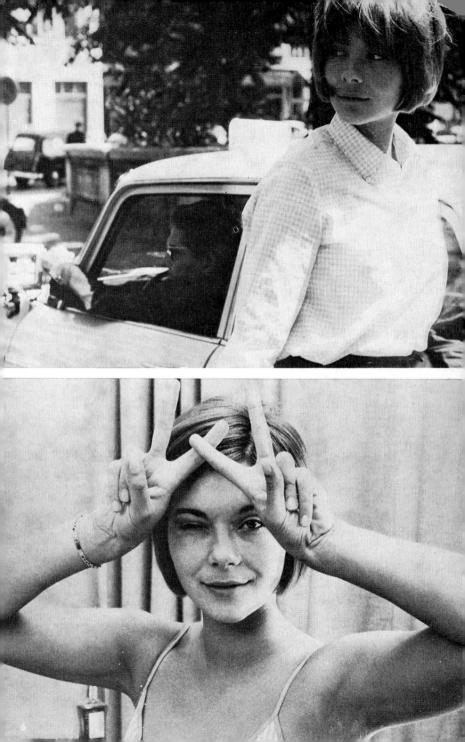

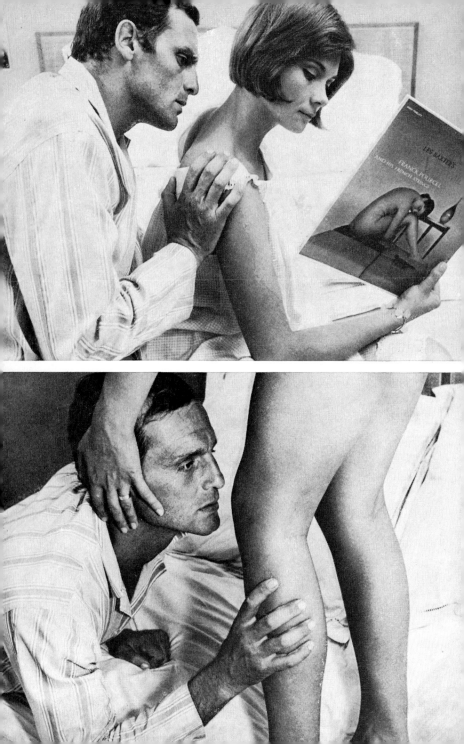

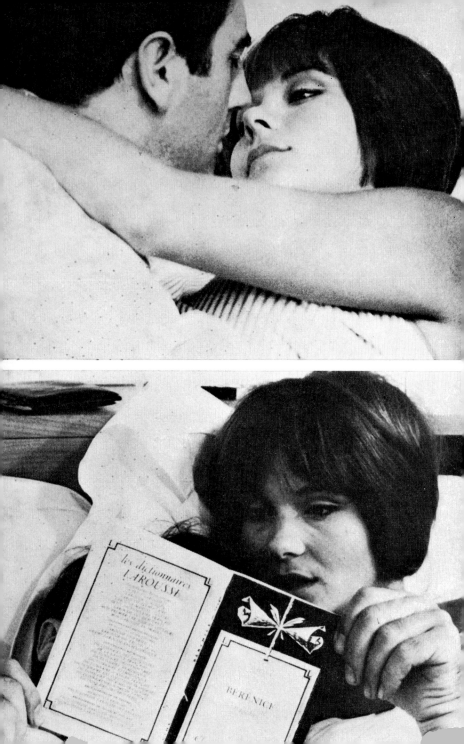

it up, looks at the number, and returns it to him. He goes off.
She runs towards the hotel reception.

TITLE:

TAKE SIDES

In the hotel bedroom, we see them in close-up. He undoes her
dress. On the corner of the wash-basin lies CHARLOTTE's
wedding-ring, as four hands soap each other. The leitmotiv
music is heard. CHARLOTTE sits in an armchair, wearing a petti-
coat. We first see her legs folded under her, then a medium
shot, showing that she has replaced the ring. Under her slip,
ROBERT's hands caress her thighs. Almost in silhouette, close-
up of their faces. They kiss.
Cut to PIERRE's head, facing us. We can see the collar of the
pyjamas he wore when we saw him with CHARLOTTE.

TITLE:

POUR VOUS MADAME
FOR YOU MADAME

COMMENTARY off: *To find a solution. Men are all the same. Very
blue eyes. For the sake of appearances. Modern life. To forget
everything.*
We see CHARLOTTE's shoulders as she takes off her clothes,
then her mouth in profile as she kisses ROBERT's forehead.
At every kiss, she murmurs an inaudible 'I love you'. The
action is repeated, with the roles reversed. Now we look down
on her, her head hanging over the edge of the bed as she lies
on her stomach. He kisses the nape of her neck, she strokes
the place he has kissed. We hear her speak over the title.

TITLE moving slowly across the screen, letter by letter:

MADAME, IF YOU LOVE YOUR HUSBAND

CHARLOTTE off: *Why does one do things? Sometimes not to make
sure that one is right, but to make sure that one is wrong.*
ROBERT is seen standing, glancing at a Larousse Classic.
CHARLOTTE off: *How soon are you going?*

113

ROBERT: *In an hour.*

She approaches and puts her bracelet on the corner shelf of the divan, while he lights a cigarette.

CHARLOTTE: *Are you insured?*

ROBERT: *Not for one hour.*

CHARLOTTE: *That doesn't matter. An hour is quite long enough to have an accident . . . and get killed.*

ROBERT: *It's all right to die in a plane crash. It's quick and there are several of you.*

They disappear into the bathroom.

CHARLOTTE off: *What did you tell me you were going to act in at Marseilles?*

ROBERT off: *A Racine play.*

We follow her as she returns with a glass of water and goes to prepare the twin beds. ROBERT has come in after her, but in a moment he goes out of our sight.

CHARLOTTE: *It's true. It's a modern death.*

ROBERT: *Oh, come off it.*

CHARLOTTE: *When I am divorced, will you marry me?*

ROBERT off: *Of course I shall.*

CHARLOTTE: *And if I have a child. . . . Will you adopt it, even if it isn't yours?*

ROBERT off: *Yes, but it will be mine. Why do you ask me that? We've discussed it a hundred times.*

CHARLOTTE: *I think that you have a funny voice.*

Pan towards ROBERT, taking off his shoes as he sits between the two beds.

ROBERT: *Who . . . me? . . . Now?*

CHARLOTTE off: *No, all the time.*

ROBERT: *I have the average male voice of the speed-age.*

CHARLOTTE off: *You haven't got the normal male voice.* She shouts at him. *You've got a coward's voice!*

ROBERT: *What's going on?*

CHARLOTTE off: *Oh nothing, I'm an idiot.*

We look down as they push the twin beds together.

CHARLOTTE: *Why do I love you? Because I do love you, you know . . .*

ROBERT: *Are you getting undressed?*

CHARLOTTE off: *Yes. Aren't you?*

114

ROBERT: *No, I'm only taking off my trousers. My Caravelle leaves in half an hour.*

CHARLOTTE is in her slip on the bed.

ROBERT off: *What did you do yesterday evening?*

CHARLOTTE is now by the window, watching an aeroplane flying overhead.

There is the sound of the posture-belt ringing.

CHARLOTTE: *Nothing. I watched T.V.*

ROBERT, wearing pants and a T-shirt, comes up and kisses her.

ROBERT: *Did you bring the seven thousand francs for the gadget?*

CHARLOTTE: *Yes. Look, here they are.*

ROBERT taking the money: *I've suddenly realized that it's the first time that we've been separated.*

He kisses her, then leans against the bay window. CHARLOTTE wanders round the room, looks through the Larousse Classic which she has picked up from the bedside shelves. She kisses him from time to time, in passing.

CHARLOTTE: *It's true, it's the first time that we're going to be any distance from each other. Out of Paris.*

ROBERT: *Don't be sad. Do you remember in the Bois de Boulogne? You said that you always straightened your back in adversity? Like that girl. . . . What's she called. . . . You know, in the American novel.*

CHARLOTTE: *Scarlet O'Hara?*

ROBERT: *I'll be terribly unhappy. Five days without you.*

Renewed kisses.

ROBERT: *What about you?*

She walks in front of him again, very relaxed.

CHARLOTTE: *Me too, because I love you. . . . But in any case, I shall find out . . .*

They clasp each other.

TITLE white letters on black screen:

7   THE THEATRE AND LOVE

CHARLOTTE off: *I've often wondered who you really are, Robert?*

ROBERT in close-up: *That's a funny question. I don't really know who I am. You know, I'm a fellow like the rest, I've got defects,*

115

like the rest . . .

CHARLOTTE off: *Tell me. You say you're an actor?*

ROBERT: *Yes, why?*

CHARLOTTE off: *What exactly is an actor?*

ROBERT: *An actor is a gentleman who gets on the stage, or, . . . and who performs. . . . He is somebody who attempts to interpret a role . . . to draw . . . to create . . . a character . . . to get outside oneself, one's own feelings and ideas.*

Close-up of CHARLOTTE.

ROBERT off: *Isn't that what you think?*

Resume on ROBERT.

CHARLOTTE off: *And at this moment?*

ROBERT: *Yes?*

CHARLOTTE off: *You're taking action in a certain situation?*

ROBERT: *Yes, at this moment I'm taking what I hope will be the right action for myself in a situation . . . in my situation, and it's not easy. . . . I'm standing up for my job as an actor, my place as a man.*

CHARLOTTE off: *How can you tell the difference between life and acting?*

Resume on CHARLOTTE.

ROBERT off: *Oh, in my opinion, in life one isn't acting. I don't feel at all as though I'm acting.* Close-up of his face. *You know, there are some chaps who . . . you can see they're acting . . . they're trying to. But I don't think I do. I may be wrong.*

CHARLOTTE off: *And what about the theatre?*

ROBERT: *Yes?*

CHARLOTTE off: *At the theatre, do you feel you exist? Or are you just a vehicle?*

ROBERT: *Well, I think. . . . It's difficult to answer that question. I think it's a bit of the two. It's undeniable that one is a vehicle, to a certain extent . . .*

CHARLOTTE off: *I'm a vehicle, but also . . .*

ROBERT: *Yes?*

CHARLOTTE off: *But if it is both, it's like this life. There's no difference between life and the theatre?*

ROBERT: *Oh yes, there is! There is a difference. . . . You're asking me questions like that, and just answering them off the cuff like this!*

CHARLOTTE off: *So therefore at this moment, it is acting?*

116

ROBERT: *No, it's not. It's different for acting . . . because there's the text . . . the play. One attempts to bring alive something which isn't personal to oneself . . . whereas, what I'm doing at this moment is . . . that you're asking me questions and I'm trying to reply as plainly as I know how. But it's my own text. I'm acting a role which is my own, which is quite different from acting a role in the theatre. You can't say I'm acting because, because . . .*

CHARLOTTE off: *When you make love, is that acting?*

ROBERT: *Oh, no! No! Certainly not! Nothing to do with it at all!*

CHARLOTTE off: *So you don't like it, then. It's not a pleasure for you?*

ROBERT smiling: *Why ever not?*

CHARLOTTE off: *Because you like acting.*

ROBERT: *But you can like acting, and you can like making love. They are two absolutely different things. Get me right.*

CHARLOTTE off: *If you had to choose, which would you choose?*

ROBERT: *Making love.* Close-up of CHARLOTTE as he repeats. *Making love.*

Resume on ROBERT, looking closely at her. The bell of the posture-belt rings.

CHARLOTTE off: *It's funny. I'm always afraid in case you're acting.*

ROBERT: *Oh no, no! Look, I promise you. You know that I love you and that when I say so I'm completely sincere, and I really think it.*

CHARLOTTE off: *But how can I know that you're completely sincere? How can I know that you're not acting?*

ROBERT: *But I've given you proof. There are concrete things which exist between us. And they're right outside the question of acting!*

CHARLOTTE off: *What does ' love ' mean to you?*

ROBERT sighing: *Love is what I feel for you.*

CHARLOTTE: *No, please think carefully before you reply.*

ROBERT: *I promise you that . . .*

CHARLOTTE off: *Think what it really means to you.*

ROBERT: *Really, love, that's what I feel for you, everything that can exist inside me for . . . that's love. That's really love.*

CHARLOTTE off: *No, don't talk about me. Talk about you.*

ROBERT: *But how can I do that? I don't know, but it seems to me that talking about love is talking about the relations between two people. You understand, love is . . . oneself in relation to somebody else? It's oneself in relation to . . . er . . . I don't know . . .*

Dissolve into darkness, from which we hear the flight announcements on the loudspeaker. As they end, we see CHARLOTTE from behind, naked. ROBERT is stroking her thighs and bottom.

FLIGHT-ANNOUNCER off: *The flight for Marseilles, Air-Inter Number 617, will depart at 17.50 hours. Will passengers please go to departure gate Number 17, by 17.30 hours.*

The announcement is repeated in English.

ROBERT's hand strokes her bottom. Darkness. Music as we come close to his face. Now we see her legs being stroked, now a close-up of the back of his head and neck with her in front of him. He kisses each of her shoulders, and we follow his mouth moving from one side to the other as they talk.

CHARLOTTE: *If I asked you what your good qualities were, what would you say?*

ROBERT: *My good qualities? Why not my faults?*

CHARLOTTE: *No. It's your good qualities that I'm interested in.*

ROBERT: *Intelligence. Distrustfulness.*

CHARLOTTE: *Is distrustfulness a quality?*

ROBERT: *Yes.*

CHARLOTTE: *Is that all?*

ROBERT: *Sincerity . . .*

CHARLOTTE: *What about loving me?*

ROBERT: *Oh yes, that's a quality. And you, what would you say your qualities are?*

CHARLOTTE: *Never to think twice about anything.*

We look down on the back of ROBERT's shirt, as he lies on top of CHARLOTTE. (*Still*) He kisses her. They turn the other way round on the bed.

CHARLOTTE: *You know, Pierre rang me yesterday from Düsseldorf? He's coming home this evening.*

ROBERT: *Will you go to bed with him?*

CHARLOTTE: *I don't know. Well, perhaps, if he asks me!*

He turns quickly towards her.

ROBERT: *What do you mean, ' perhaps '?*

CHARLOTTE: *Could you kiss two girls at the same time, caress them?*

ROBERT: *I'd have to choose, too.*

He strokes her calves.

FLIGHT-ANNOUNCER off: *The flight for Marseilles Air-Inter Number*

118

617 is about to depart. Will passengers please go immediately to Gate 17.

Again, the announcement is repeated in English.

From above, we see them both lying down. ROBERT's face is hidden by the Larousse Classic, which he is reading dramatically. (*Still*)

ROBERT: ' *Spare me, Madame, Unfortunate prince that I am,*
Both of us cannot give way to our feelings here . . .'

He lowers the book and looks at CHARLOTTE.

ROBERT: *You give me my cues.*

CHARLOTTE: *Er . . . um.*

ROBERT starting to read again:

' *And if I ever do avoid what I feel, but too late,*
These cruel conversations in which I have no part . . .'

He looks across to CHARLOTTE.

ROBERT: *It's you now.*

CHARLOTTE reading:

' *I myself wanted to listen to you in this spot.*
I will listen no more, good-bye for ever! '

ROBERT carrying on:

' *So how can I put it, finally? I flee from the abstracted glance,*
Which, though always turned in my direction, never sees me.
Goodbye! I. . . . A pause.
Go, my mind is too full of your image,
To wait for death while loving you
Above all do not fear . . .
Above all do not fear. A pause. That I shall be so blinded by grief
That I will fill the world with the reason for it . . .
The only thing that will remind you I was alive,
Will be the report of my death, which I hope may come soon.'

CHARLOTTE reading:

' *For ever, oh my lord, think, deep in yourself,*
How terrible this cruel world is when one loves,
What shall we be suffering in a month, in a year, my lord?
When so many seas separate me from you,
When the day begins, and the day ends
But Titus will never see Berenice again? '

Darkness, then, in the same shot which opened the film, we

119

look down on the white sheet. CHARLOTTE's hand slides across it.

ROBERT off: *Are you crying?*

CHARLOTTE off: *No I'm not, what makes you say that?*

ROBERT off: *You've got tears in your eyes.*

CHARLOTTE off: *Yes, I'm crying.*

ROBERT off: *Come on, it's over.*

He withdraws his hand. It remains on top of CHARLOTTE's on the sheet.

ROBERT off: *I must go.*

Very slowly, CHARLOTTE's hand slides out of sight below the base of the screen.

CHARLOTTE off: *Yes . . . yes. . . . It's over . . .*

THE END

TWO OR THREE THINGS
I KNOW ABOUT HER

CREDITS:

Production Company	Anouchka Films/Argos Films/ Les Films du Carrosse/Parc Film (Paris)
Production Manager	Philippe Senné
Director	Jean-Luc Godard
Assistant Directors	Charles Bitsch
	Isabelle Pons
Script	Jean-Luc Godard
Director of Photography	Raoul Coutard
Camera Operator	Georges Liron
Editors	Françoise Collin
	Chantal Delattre
Sound	René Levert
	Antoine Bonfanti
Narrator	Jean-Luc Godard
Costumes	Gitt Marrini

CAST:

Juliette Janson	Marina Vlady
Marianne	Anny Duperey
Robert Janson	Roger Montsoret
Roger	Jean Narboni
Christophe	Christophe Bourseiller
Solange	Marie Bourseiller
John Bogus	Raoul Lévy
Monsieur Gérard	Joseph Gehrard

TWO OR THREE THINGS I KNOW ABOUT HER

The credits appear on the screen.
TITLE red, white and blue letters:

VISA DE CONTROLE CINEMATOGRAPHIQUE 32 167

The numbers 2, and OR 3, flash on screen several times in quick succession to the loud sound of pneumatic drills.
TITLE red, white and blue letters:

THINGS I KNOW ABOUT HER
HER, THE PARIS REGION

We now move to the Paris region, by a large housing estate on a sunny day. Long shot, tilting down onto a vast building site with a link road. On the road, a wheelbarrow.
Mobile cranes are emptying their loads. There are loud construction noises coming from the site.
Another long shot of a large housing estate just like any on the outskirts of Paris. This shot is held while Jean-Luc Godard speaks off, in a low, even whisper, which is barely audible above the various sounds.
COMMENTARY off: *On August 19, the Journal Officiel published a decree relating to the organization of State services in the Paris Region. Two days later, the Council of Ministers appointed Paul Delouvrier préfet of the Paris Region . . .* long shot of the housing estate shopping-centre with people hurrying to and fro . . . *which, according to the Ministry of Information communiqué, will give the Region a specific and coherent orientation.*
Medium close-up of JULIETTE-MARINA VLADY. Her back is turned to the light and she appears to be standing on the balcony of her own flat in the middle of the housing estate. Beyond, to her left, another block of flats.
COMMENTARY continued off: *That's Marina Vlady. She's an actress.*

123

She's wearing a blue-grey sweater with two yellow stripes. She's of Russian descent. Her hair may be light or dark brown, I'm not quite sure which.

MARINA pats her hair and stares into camera, then lowers her eyes.

MARINA: *Yes, to speak as though one were quoting the truth. Old Brecht said so. That actors must quote.*

Sound of children playing. New shot of MARINA-JULIETTE, medium close-up, almost identical except that she now faces the left-hand side of the screen while the block of flats in the background is to the right.

COMMENTARY continued off: *She now looks right, not that it matters. And it's Juliette Janson. She lives here. She's wearing a blue-grey sweater with two yellow stripes. Her hair may be light or dark brown, I'm not quite sure which. She's of Russian descent.*

JULIETTE: *Two years ago in Martinique. Exactly like in a Simenon novel. No, I don't know which one . . . , yes,* Banana Tourists, *that's the one. I have to manage somehow. Robert earns one hundred and ten thousand francs a month, I think.*

COMMENTARY off: *Now she turns her head to the left . . . she does not turn . . . but it doesn't matter . . . she turns her head to the left.*

Camera tilts up in long shot of two cranes, a red one and a white one, outlined against the clear blue sky. Loud noises. The cranes move so that they cross each other in mid-air.

The commentary opens on different shots of the housing estate: a garage with the conspicuous sign: AZUR. A shopping centre in the housing estate, seen through the window of a furniture shop. A supermarket.

COMMENTARY off: *I've already worked out that Paul Delouvrier,[1] in spite of his fine-sounding name, began his career in the Lazard and Rothschild banking trusts. Which presumably means that the Gaullist regime, while claiming to modernize and to reform the system, in fact only wishes to record and to regulate the natural course of major capitalism. I also deduce that stratifying the directive and centralizing processes, the same authority accentuates the distortion of the national economy, and still more that of the underlying day by day morality.*

---

[1] Delouvrier — de l'ouvrier — of the worker. Translator's note.

Close-up of a book by Raymond Aron published in the *Idées* series.[1]

TITLE:

DIX-HUIT LECONS
SUR LA SOCIETE
INDUSTRIELLE

We move to the living room of the Jansons' flat, it is evening.
JULIETTE off: *What am I looking at? . . . The floor. That's all. I can feel the table cloth under my hand.*
Children's voices.
Close-up of the inside of a transmitting and receiving set, showing red, blue and yellow wires, white plugs and a grey amplifier. Wisps of smoke from the cigarettes of two men talking off. They are ROBERT, JULIETTE's husband, and ROGER, his friend. Both men are enthusiastic radio amateurs.
ROBERT off: *Incredible!*
ROGER off: *Can you hear anything?*
ROBERT off: *Yes.*
ROGER off: *What is it?*
ROBERT off: *It's between Saigon and Washington.*
Medium long shot of a section of the living room with the table and the radio. ROBERT smoking a cigarette, is sitting with his back to the camera, eagerly listening to the radio with earphones while ROGER, in profile, sits next to him. On the wall behind them hangs a poster of the film *Muriel* by Alain Resnais and Jean Cayrol. Near the table, a teddy-bear and, in the right-hand corner of the screen, a green rubber plant reaching to the ceiling.
JULIETTE, who has been sitting with her elbow on the table, now gets up and leaves.
JULIETTE off: *I say, Christophe, what are you doing?*
ROGER to ROBERT: *Who is talking?*
ROBERT: *Johnson.*
ROGER: *Johnson? Johnson. Well, what's he saying?*
ROBERT repeating aloud what he hears: ' *It was with a heavy heart*

---

[1] The paperback Idées series, published by Gallimard, recurs in inserts throughout the film.

125

*that I gave orders to my pilots to bomb North Vietnam in 1965,
to bring Hanoi to the negotiating table . . .'*
ROGER: *Go on . . .*

Off screen, barely audible because the two men are talking
loudly, JULIETTE sounds as though she is scolding her son.

ROBERT: *' They did a great job! . . . But Hanoi refused to negotiate.
So that in 1966, again with a heavy heart, I gave orders to my
pilots to bomb Haiphong and Hanoi . . .'*
ROGER: *Let me listen a moment.*

ROBERT gives the earphones to ROGER.

Off screen, Christophe is reciting his homework, there is a
sound of whimpering.

ROGER repeating what he hears: *' They did a great job, but Hanoi
did not come to the negotiating table. So that in July 67, still with
a heavy heart, I asked my pilots to destroy the Chinese atomic
installations. They did a great job, but Hanoi refused to negotiate.'*

He takes off the earphones and gives them back to ROBERT.

JULIETTE reappears and sits down next to her husband, she
starts reading the weekly magazine l'Express.

ROBERT: *' In 1967, to make Hanoi negotiate, it was with a heavy
heart that I ordered my pilots to bomb Peking . . .'*
ROGER: *Go on . . .*
ROBERT: *' They did a great job but Hanoi refused to negotiate.
Now my rockets are directed on Moscow . . .'*
ROGER: *Go on . . .*
ROBERT: *President Johnson declares, ' Hanoi must realize . . . that
my patience is coming to an end.'* Close-up of the radio set. *Oh
shit! I can't hear a thing now.*

ROBERT tries to fix the radio, while JULIETTE turns over the
pages of l'Express. *(Still)*

JULIETTE: *Hey . . . wouldn't you like it if I ' slipped into a pair of
fake anklets or knee socks printed on tights designed by Louis
Ferraud. They make an indecent dress look modest and are amusing
as well as charming as long as your legs are perfectly slim and
youthful-looking.'*
ROBERT to JULIETTE: *Oh stop talking nonsense!*
JULIETTE: *It's in Madame Express!*
ROBERT: *Never heard of it.*
JULIETTE shrugging: *You're illiterate!* She leaves the two men and

we hear her talking, off. *Okay, kids, come and say goodnight.* CHRISTOPHE, who is aged about ten, appears and gives his father and ROGER a goodnight kiss. JULIETTE comes on screen carrying SOLANGE, a little girl of about four years of age. *Say goodnight to Daddy.*

They leave and the men go back to their radio set.

ROBERT: *Some American generals are speaking now.*

ROGER: *What are they saying?*

ROBERT: *That they want to bomb North Vietnam back to the Stone Age . . . calling out . . . That's what stone means, doesn't it, Juliette?*

JULIETTE off: *Yes.*

Pause. We can hear SOLANGE crying, off.

ROGER to ROBERT: *Tell me, how did you pay for your Austin?*

ROBERT: *Oh, Juliette found it. Yes, she's marvellous, always turns up bargains.*

ROGER: *That's great! I need a woman like that, who can manage on her own.*

Close-up of the radio set and the cigarette smoke.

Loud whine of aeroplane and crash of bombs falling.

TITLE red and blue letters:

> MADE IN
> U.S.A.
> PRISUNIC
> FROM APRIL 16

COMMENTARY over title, off: *Oh, dear George Washington, what on earth made you want to play the part of cruel William Pitt?*

Close-up of the radio set and the cigarette smoke which looks like the smoke-clouds made by an explosion. The sound of bombs and machine-gun fire. Whine of planes dive-bombing.

TITLE red letters on white:[1]

> PAX

COMMENTARY over title off, louder than before: *Pax Americana. . . . Super bargain-size brain-washing . . .*

We move to JULIETTE's kitchen, where she is standing with her

---

[1] This insert is a close-up of a well-known brand of detergent.

back to us, washing up the dishes. The sink is cluttered with various washing-up products: BONUX, MIR, JAVEL, etc. On the right a German poster of Buster Keaton standing upside down.

JULIETTE: *A kind of ' message from beyond '. . . . I was washing the dishes and I started to cry. I heard a voice saying to me: ' You are indestructible '. I, me, myself, everyone.*

A few chords of music.

ROBERT calling off: *Juliette! Juliette!*

JULIETTE: *Time is very confusing. I don't understand very well. No, there's no need to find a definition.*

ROBERT calling off: *Juliette! Roger's leaving!*

JULIETTE calling back: *Yes, coming!* To camera. *One often tries to understand, to define the meaning of a word, but it's too confusing. One must acknowledge that it's much easier to look upon such and such a thing as self-evident.*

TITLE blue letters on yellow:

IDEES

COMMENTARY over: *One thing is obvious that the structuring of the Paris Region will enable the government to carry out its class policy with even greater ease.*

Blurred colours gradually sharpening into focus until we see what is either a painting or a photograph of a bunch of flowers. Camera zooms back and we realize that it is a postcard lying on the grass.

COMMENTARY continued: *And that the monopolies will be able to direct and to organize the economy without really taking into account the aspirations to a better life of those eight million inhabitants.*

Outside a housing estate during the day, the camera pans slowly from one half-built block of flats, to some finished ones. Construction noises from the building site fill the background.

In the Jansons' bedroom, JULIETTE is lying in bed with her eyes shut. The sheets are white, the blanket red and JULIETTE wears a blue sweater.

JULIETTE: *The eyes are the body . . . and noise is . . .*

There is a knock at the door. She opens her eyes.

128

Sound of a door opening, off.

CHRISTOPHE off: *Mummy, listen, do you ever have dreams?*

JULIETTE: *Hurry up, you'll be late for school.*

CHRISTOPHE off: *I want to know.*

JULIETTE: *When I used to dream, I would feel as though I were being sucked into a big hole, as though a big hole were swallowing me up . . .* she lets her head fall back on the pillow. *. . . Now I feel as though I were being shattered into a million pieces when I dream . . .* pause. *. . . And when I used to wake up, before, even when it took a long time, I'd wake up all in one piece. Now, when I wake up, I'm scared some of the bits will be missing.*

CHRISTOPHE off: *Mummy, I had a dream last night, you know.*

JULIETTE: *What did you dream about?*

Close-up of CHRISTOPHE, standing by the half-open door, rubbing his eye. He speaks with a slight lisp.

CHRISTOPHE: *Well, I dreamt I was walking all by myself down a road next to a precipice. There was only room for one person.* Pause. *Then all of a sudden I saw two twins walking ahead of me . . . so I wondered how they would manage to pass when suddenly one . . . one of the twins moved towards . . .* he rubs his eye *. . . the other . . . , and merged into him . . . and they turned into one person. And then I realized that these . . . these two people . . . were North and South Vietnam . . . reuniting.* Close-up of JULIETTE. *Mummy, what does language mean?*

JULIETTE in close-up: *Language is the house in which man dwells.*

Music. She pats her hair and rests her head on the pillow.

Close-up of a comic strip in garish colours showing a girl in the foreground with a Bentley in the background close to her. Beyond, a chain of bluish mountains with snow-capped peaks.

TITLE book jacket:

DES CLASSES
NOUVELLES LECONS
SUR LES SOCIETES INDUSTRIELLES

A bathroom in a housing estate. A pretty Hungarian girl sits in a bathtub, her naked body partially covered by bubble-bath. Her breasts are whiter than the rest of her suntanned body. The washbasin next to the tub is littered with cosmetics. The girl, remaining seated, takes a pink facecloth from the washbasin and starts washing herself. She puts down the facecloth and picks up a headband which she puts round her head. She then turns on a tap which is connected to a flexible rubber hose, feels the water to check the temperature and gets up. She stands with her back to the camera, washing herself. There is a knock on the door. The girl seems to ask who it is but her voice is muffled by the sound of running water. She turns the hand-shower off and puts it down to grab a towel which she puts in front of her body just as an Electricity Board employee walks in, giving her a little salute. We recognize him by his cap.

ELECTRICITY BOARD EMPLOYEE: *Hello, Miss . . .* the girl screams and bursts into a flood of Hungarian, the man talks above this. . . . *Electricity Board. Where's the meter?* He walks past her then returns carrying a meter log-book. *Dear me you're going to hate this. . . . Fifty thousand francs to pay!*

He jots down the figures in his meter log-book while the girl continues to yell at him.

The outside of a housing estate. In the foreground on the left, the last two letters of a big sign: A L. On the right, a block of flats.

COMMENTARY off: *If you suddenly have luxuries you never had before, you start to overspend and . . .*

Close-up of a rather sad looking girl, facing the camera. Her lips do not move, yet she seems to be saying the words spoken in an undertone by Jean-Luc Godard, off. Very blurred neon signs in the background. The girl appears to be standing in the shopping centre of the housing estate. It is evening. The background is deliberately left out of focus.

COMMENTARY continued off: *. . . hot water, without thinking that you'll have to pay the bill at the end of the month. Always the same old story! No money to pay for the rent, or else no television set, or else a television set but no car, or else a washing-machine but no holidays.*

A building site. A crane moves in the sky. In the foreground, a sign with the word AZUR written on it in huge letters.

COMMENTARY continued off: *Not a normal life in other words.*

MR. GERARD's flat in the housing estate. MR. GERARD is looking out of the window at the street. He is a man in his early fifties, he wears a check shirt, an old striped pullover and a rather grubby felt hat. There are various travel posters around the walls. He finally turns away from the window and the camera pans after him as he walks towards a door which has travel posters of Bangkok and Israel on either side of it. He opens the door so that we see a couple reclining on a couch inside the room. The man, who is dressed like a worker, is stroking the girl's thighs. She is obviously a casual prostitute, about eighteen years old. On the wall behind them, a travel poster of Japan. In the foreground, his back turned to the camera, MR GERARD looks at his watch. He walks into the room, disappears, then comes back. As he leaves the room, he speaks.

MR. GERARD: *Only seven minutes to go.*

He shuts the door and the front door-bell rings.

He goes down the small hallway and opens the front door.

MR. GERARD: *Good afternoon, Mrs. Janson.*

JULIETTE comes in, holding her daughter, SOLANGE, by the hand. SOLANGE is crying bitterly.

JULIETTE: *Hello, Mr Gerard. I've brought Solange.*

SOLANGE screaming and stammering: *Oh! . . . euh! Mummy! Mummy!*

JULIETTE drags SOLANGE towards the sitting-room where three other children, two boys and a girl, are playing. There is a coloured poster of Anna Karina in *Vivre sa Vie* on the wall. Leaving her daughter with the other children JULIETTE walks back towards the front door. MR. GERARD hurries after her.

MR. GERARD: *Excuse me! . . . Mrs. Janson. . . . Aren't you forgetting something?*

JULIETTE off: *Oh yes!*

JULIETTE gives MR. GERARD a bar of chocolate. He takes it. Little SOLANGE swallowing her tears, tries to slip past them and creeps unnoticed towards the front door.

JULIETTE: *Here. . . . It's all I've got, but next week I'll let you have some more. Well, goodbye.*

She rushes towards the door, pushes the weeping SOLANGE out of the way and leaves. MR. GERARD closes the door and gently pushes the little girl in the direction of the sitting-room. He looks at his watch in annoyance and points towards the room where SOLANGE must go, urging her to join the other children.

131

He then puts the chocolate down on a table with some other sweets.

MR. GERARD: *Go over there with the others.*

MR. GERARD goes and opens the door which he opened at the beginning of the scene. The man and woman are still there, lying on the couch.

MR. GERARD: *Only three minutes left.*

SOLANGE stands behind him whimpering. He closes the door and is about to lead the little girl away when the doorbell rings again. He opens the front door, a young woman comes in.

YOUNG WOMAN: *Hello, Mr. Gerard, may we come in?*

MR. GERARD: *Yes . . . , this way.*

He points to another door. The woman goes through followed by a young man who gives MR. GERARD something as he walks past him. SOLANGE's head is visible in the foreground.

YOUNG MAN: *I could only find toffee!*

MR. GERARD follows them through the door and vanishes.

SOLANGE still weeping: *Mummy! I want my Mummy!*

MR. GERARD comes out by another door, alone. He goes and sits on a couch next to the children and holds out his arms to SOLANGE. SOLANGE moves towards him.

MR. GERARD: *Come over here with the other children. Come along. Come, we'll play together. Come on, I'll read you a story.* He picks up a children's book. *Come on, we'll read you a nice story, come here, little one.*

Down in the street below, from the window, JULIETTE is seen looking at a policeman who is leading away two manacled long-haired youths. Several children are following them, out of curiosity. JULIETTE finally walks away.

MR. GERARD off: *There, sit down here. I'll read you a little story. Pic and Pouc. . . . Pic and Pouc walk along the river bank. Mrs. Pelican is hatching . . . hatching some eggs . . .*

Outside, Paris. A succession of long shots gradually leads us into the heart of the city. New roads are under construction, a barge moves along a canal, long shot of the Seine, in the Neuilly-Courbevoie-Puteaux area. Loud construction noises and pneumatic drills. The commentary begins on a medium close-up of a girl, facing camera. She leans against a street hoarding, which is covered with brightly coloured bill posters, smoking a cigarette.

COMMENTARY off: *It's always the same story. Apprentice seamstress, she left school and got a job in a small workshop. She met a boy who got her pregnant and then walked out on her. A year later, she had another child by a different man who also left her.* A man wearing glasses, stops in front of the girl, talks to her, then moves on; camera remains on her as she looks away. *They lectured her at the maternity hospital but that was also where some girl-friends told her how to earn enough money to feed her two kids. When she left, she went back to her old job but in the evening she would go out on the streets. Then she was lucky enough to meet a nice fellow who fell in love with her and they got married.*

The girl stares into the camera.

A wide Paris street on a sunny day. The red, blue and yellow hoardings in front of a demolition site are not yet covered with posters, so they seem to glow in the light. Cars and people stream past.

COMMENTARY off: *They move into a modern flat with the kids. Needless to say, the rent is too high. Two years later, a third child. They can't make ends meet and it's the husband himself who sends his wife out on the streets.*

JULIETTE walks up some stairs which lead into the shop, called VOG. She looks at the clothes and takes off her blue striped raincoat. She goes over to the shirt counter where two young salesgirls are standing. JULIETTE chooses a striped shirt, and facing the camera, holds it up to herself. There is a deafening noise of traffic coming from the street outside.

JULIETTE: *Is this cotton?*

FIRST SALESGIRL coming into shot: *Yes it is.*

JULIETTE puts down the shirt and continues looking at the other clothes. She goes over to some dresses which are hanging side by side and points to some red material.

JULIETTE to another salesgirl: *Have you got any dresses in this material?*

SECOND SALESGIRL: *Yes, Madam, on the second floor.*

JULIETTE: *Thank you.*

The SECOND SALESGIRL comes up to the camera, talking to us in the same tone she used to JULIETTE. The latter remains slightly out of focus in the background looking at dresses.

133

SECOND SALESGIRL: *I'm knocking off work at seven and meeting Jean-Claude at eight. We go to the restaurant, sometimes to a film.*
The SALESGIRL walks away and JULIETTE goes up to a small fashion poster: *Jardin des Modes.* She then picks out a skirt and goes over to a mirror, talking aloud to the camera.
JULIETTE: *Yes, I know how to talk. All right, let's talk together.*[1]
Flash on the link road. *Together in a group. Group. . . . I like that word.* Resume on JULIETTE. *A group of buildings means thousands of people, maybe a whole town.* Loud noise from within the shop. *No one today can know what the cities of tomorrow will be like. They will definitely lose some of their cultural heritage. Definitely.* She looks straight at the camera, pause, silence. *Perhaps other methods of communication will replace the creative and formative role once played by the city . . . , perhaps. . . . Television, Radio, Vocabularly and Syntax, deliberately and scientifically . . .*
Two SALESGIRLS are standing behind the sweater counter, chatting together as they sort through their merchandise.
THIRD SALESGIRL to camera: *It's three o'clock. I haven't eaten lunch yet.* To herself, *Navy-blue shetland.*
JULIETTE off: *They'll have to invent a new language.*
THIRD SALESGIRL to camera: *I got up at eight o'clock. My eyes are hazel . . .*
TITLE book jacket:

PSYCHOLOGIE
DE LA FORME

Resume on JULIETTE, still in the shop, walking past a fashion publicity poster, *Chosen by Vogue.* Another salesgirl, her back turned to camera, walks up to JULIETTE.
FOURTH SALESGIRL: *Can I help you, Madam?*
JULIETTE absent-mindedly: *Can I try this on?*
FOURTH SALESGIRL: *Of course.*
JULIETTE goes and selects a white fur coat, and walks over to the mirror. (*Still*)
JULIETTE aloud to herself: *In this room, the colours are red, green and blue.* She comes back to hang up the coat. *Yes I'm sure of that.*

---

[1] Pun on the word ' ensemble ' which means together and housing estate. Translator's note.

She goes up to another fur coat and takes it off the hanger. *I'm wearing a blue sweater.*

> She holds the coat up in front of herself and looks into a mirror.

FOURTH SALESGIRL: *The white one looks very good on you.*

JULIETTE: *What I'm looking for is a cotton dress with sleeves.*

FOURTH SALESGIRL putting away the white coat: *Yes, I'll show you.*

> JULIETTE goes to the dress department.

JULIETTE: *Because I can see it's blue.*

FOURTH SALESGIRL: *This way please.*

> JULIETTE follows the salesgirl who is now showing her a pink striped dress. She holds the dress up in front of herself and looks into a mirror.

JULIETTE aloud to herself: *If they'd got it wrong in the first place and they had called blue green . . . that would be a serious matter.* To the SALESGIRL: *All right, this one will do. The trouble is. What time do you shut?*

> She gives back the dress.

FOURTH SALESGIRL: *At seven o'clock.*

JULIETTE: *Can you put it aside for me and I'll come back later because . . .*

FOURTH SALESGIRL: *I really can't keep it for you.*

JULIETTE: *Why not?*

FOURTH SALESGIRL: *Well, ask the . . .*

> She points off and the camera follows JULIETTE, who picks up her raincoat and her handbag and goes over to where the manageress sits behind a desk.

JULIETTE: *Can you keep it for me for an hour or two? I've got to go to the bank.*

THE MANAGERESS: *Certainly, Madam. No later than six.*

JULIETTE: *I'll be back before six.*

THE MANAGERESS: *Very well then.*

> JULIETTE slips on her raincoat and starts to leave the shop, then stops.

JULIETTE to camera: *It's because my impressions aren't always precise. Take desire for instance. I know sometimes what it is I desire. At other times, I don't know. For example, I know there's something missing in my life, but I don't really know what. Or else I feel scared though there's nothing particular to be frightened about.*

Pause. *Which expressions are not related to any specific objects?
Ah yes! Order. Logic. Yes, for example, something can make me cry,
but . . . but the reason for those tears is not directly connected
with the actual tears that trickle down my cheeks. In other words,
everything I do can be described but not necessarily the reasons for
which I do it.* She turns to the manageress who is off-screen. *I'll
be back at six.*

Noises from the street outside grow louder.

Cut to a road in the process of construction.

The noise is deafening. There are some workers operating a
concrete mixer.

Silence.

COMMENTARY off: *I study the life of the city and of the city-dwellers,
their interrelationship, as minutely as the biologist studies the
interrelationship which exists between the individual and the race
during the evolutionary stages.*

Street with coloured hoardings concealing buildings in the
process of demolition. Long shot of JULIETTE crossing the
street, walking towards camera then out of shot.

COMMENTARY off: *That is the only way I can really deal with the
pathological state in which society finds itself and start to hope
for a truly new concept of urbanization.*

The ring road under construction. A lorry empties its load of
gravel. Two workers painting some railings busily.

Inside a café. JULIETTE walks in from the glassed-in terrace,
past a young man playing at a pin-ball machine, and up to the
bar where a woman is making a telephone call. JULIETTE
shakes hands with the barman who is off-screen.

BARMAN off: *Hello.*

JULIETTE: *Hello.* She walks towards the camera. *Definition of
myself, in a word: indifference.*

A FRIEND off: *Hello there!*

JULIETTE goes over to where her friend is sitting.

She shakes hands with the woman and sits down at her table.

JULIETTE: *Hello.*

The friend does not pay much attention to JULIETTE and goes
on reading a book. The pin-ball makes a lot of noise, off.

JULIETTE after a moment: *How are you?*

FRIEND looking up: *All right.* She looks down again at her book. *I*

136

came here this morning. I'll be staying for a while. I'm expecting Jean-Paul.

JULIETTE: *Oh. I'll hang around until this evening.* Calling out to the barman. *Do you sell Winstons?*

> JULIETTE gets up and goes to the bar. The friend follows her with her eyes. A GIRL is perched on a stool next to the bar. A man wearing glasses, walks by the GIRL, accompanied by another woman. He exchanges glances with the GIRL at the bar and she watches him walk past.

THE GIRL to the man: *I see you've got some new shoes!* To the camera. *I live in those blocks of flats near the Southern motorway.* She inhales her cigarette. *I come into Paris twice a month, you know, the big blue and white blocks.*

JULIETTE off: *One packet of Winstons, please, and some matches.*

> The glassed-in terrace and the young man playing at the pinball machine.

BARMAN giving JULIETTE the cigarettes and matches: *Yes, Miss . . . Madam.*

> In the foreground, her back to the light, JULIETTE thanks the barman and opens the packet of cigarettes.
>
> She then walks over to the juke-box and glances at the song-titles. She raises a cigarette to her lips, and lights it.

YOUNG MAN WITH GLASSES off: *Yes, they're American shoes.*

A GIRL off: *Are those the kind Americans use for stamping on the feet of the Vietnamese?*

YOUNG MAN WITH GLASSES off: *. . . and on the feet of South Americans too.*

> JULIETTE walks towards the camera so that we see her in close-up. Then shot of the young man with glasses who is having a drink at the bar with his woman companion.
>
> He grabs JULIETTE by the arm as she walks past them.

YOUNG MAN WITH GLASSES: *I believe we've met.*

JULIETTE annoyed: *Yeah . . .*

> She tries to move on but he holds her back.

YOUNG MAN WITH GLASSES: *Don't talk to me like that! You still don't want me to look after you? Only ten percent.* (Still)

JULIETTE: *Sure, I've heard that one before!*

YOUNG MAN WITH GLASSES: *Ask Colette . . .* he points to his companion . . . *what happened to Isabelle.*

137

JULIETTE: *I know. Someone slashed her in the face with a razor.*
YOUNG MAN WITH GLASSES: *Doesn't that scare you?*
JULIETTE: *First of all, the war's over. . . . Besides, I'm just doing this temporarily. I hope to stop soon.* She walks away. He drinks up his beer and we can hear him talking off. *Can I have a coke please?*
BARMAN off: *Yes, Madam.*

> Return to JULIETTE. She is sitting with her elbows on the table, near a young couple at another table. The woman at the next table smokes a cigarette and looks dreamily into space. The man opens his newspaper, France-Soir, and we can read the headline on the first page: 'PEKING SABOTAGES DE GAULLE-HO-CHI-MINH MEETING.' To the left of the screen, next to JULIETTE, a waiter pours out her Coca-Cola into a glass. When he leaves, she starts jotting down something in a small diary, then puts it back into her handbag. Close-up of JULIETTE. Loud noise of pin-ball machine flippers. (*Still*) JULIETTE drinks slowly, staring at the couple next to her.
> Close-up of the magazine Lui. The young woman at the next table, off, is leafing through the pages of Lui so that we see suggestive pictures of women talking out of comic-strip type balloons, though we cannot make out the text.

COMMENTARY off: *That was how Juliette, at 3.37 p.m. came to be looking at the turning pages of an object which, in journalistic jargon, is known as ' magazine '.* Close-up of the young woman who is turning over the pages of Lui. *And that was how, about one hundred and fifty pages further on, another young woman, like her in every way, a kindred spirit, a sister, was also gazing at the same object.* Close-up of the turning pages. *Where then does truth reside? In full face or in profile? And anyway what is an object?*

> Resume on the young woman who smiles rather scornfully as she turns over the pages of the magazine. Throughout the following commentary, a succession of close-ups of JULIETTE as she gazes at the couple, and of the man (in profile) as he smokes and sometimes turns to stare back at JULIETTE, and of the young woman who does not seem to mind JULIETTE's glances and her companion's interest in JULIETTE, though she has noticed both.
> Resume on JULIETTE, now alternating with close-ups of a

cup of coffee.

COMMENTARY off: *Perhaps an object can provide a link, can enable one to go from one subject to another and so to live within society, to be together. But then, given the fact that social relationships are always ambiguous, given the fact that my thoughts create rifts as much as they unite, given the fact that my words establish contacts by being spoken and create isolation by remaining unspoken, given the fact that there is such a vast gap between the subjective certainty I have of myself and the objective reality that I represent to others, given the fact that I always find myself guilty although I feel I am innocent.*

A spoon is stirring up the cup of coffee. It is withdrawn. A small circle of foam is left swirling round on the surface.

COMMENTARY continued off: *Given the fact that each event changes my day to day existence and given the fact that I invariably fail to communicate. . . . I mean to understand, to love, to be loved, and as each failure makes me feel my loneliness more keenly, as . . .*

JULIETTE stops staring at the couple and turns to look towards the bar.

The barman who wears dark glasses, is filling a glass. Constant sound of pin-ball machine flippers. The barman feels JULIETTE looking at him, and stares back.

Close-up of beer taps and of the barman's hands.

The coffee cup. Foam swirls round on the surface.

COMMENTARY off: *. . . as . . . as I cannot bring myself to give up the objectivity which oppresses me or the subjectivity which makes me feel an exile, as I can neither raise myself to a level of being nor allow myself to sink into nothingness. I must go on listening. I must go on looking about me even more keenly than in the past. The world. A kindred spirit . . . my brother.*

Close-up of the man looking at JULIETTE. Resume on the coffee.

A lump of sugar sinks like a cluster of crystals. The screen is now black, and strewn with silvery bubbles and foam.

COMMENTARY off: *Where does it begin? But where does what begin? God created the heavens and the earth. Of course, but that's an easy way out. There must be a better way of explaining it all. . . . To think that speech is as limited as the world. That the frontiers of my speech are the frontiers of my world. And that whatever I say must impose limitations on the world, must make it finite. And when logical, mysterious death comes to abolish that frontier, and when there will be no questions and no answers, everything will be blurred. Yet it will only be with the re-emergence of consciousness that it may all grow clear again. After that, everything will fall into place.*

The picture, out of focus at first, has grown progressively sharper. The music grows louder.

JULIETTE is now seen walking down an avenue in Paris, on a sunny day. Cut to her walking further down the same street. Cut to yet another shot of her walking further along still. She crosses a square. The music is very loud.

JULIETTE: *I don't know where or when. I just remember that it happened. All day, I had been searching for the feeling. I could smell the trees. I was the world. The world was me. The landscape is like a face.*

She goes off-screen. The music stops.

A building site where heavy work is in progress.

The noise is deafening.

Inside a sleazy hotel room. On the wall, a poster: SEVILLA. JULIETTE walks into the room, carrying a towel; behind her, a young man with fair hair walks in, shuts the door and casually takes off his jacket. JULIETTE puts down the towel, goes up to the young man and holds out her hand. (*Still*) He gives her some money which she slips into her handbag.

JULIETTE: *Thanks.*

YOUNG MAN: *This must be a hotel for Jews only.*

JULIETTE locking the door: *Why?*

YOUNG MAN: *It's got a star.*

JULIETTE tosses something onto the partition which divides the room into two sections: in one section, the bed, in the other, a washbasin. JULIETTE starts to wash her hands.

Next to the mirror over the washbasin, there is a poster: SAN FRANCISCO. JULIETTE turns around to say something to the young man who is off-screen.

JULIETTE: *Don't watch me undress.*

YOUNG MAN off: *Why not?*

JULIETTE: *Because I don't want you to.*

YOUNG MAN off: *You'll be naked in a minute.*

140

JULIETTE: *That's not the same thing.*

We catch sight of the young man in the mirror. (*Still*)
TITLE from ' Idées ' series:

INTRODUCTION
A L'ETHNOLOGIE

YOUNG MAN during insert off: *I come from Paris. I work in the metro. There are two million Parisians down there with me . . .*
Resume on the hotel room; the young man is unscrewing a large mirror from the wall near a JAPAN poster.
JULIETTE walks into shot and we see another poster for the *Contes de la Lune Vague.*
YOUNG MAN continued: *. . . but you never see them because taking photographs is prohibited by the police.*
He takes down the mirror and manages to set it upright on an armchair near the bed. He then sits down on the bed, facing the mirror.
YOUNG MAN: *Do you mind if I put the mirror here?*
JULIETTE combs her hair in the mirror above the washbasin.
JULIETTE: *Of course not. It isn't my fault if I have a passive streak in my nature.*
She walks about the room and then leans against the wall, next to a Japanese print, looking into the camera. (*Still*)
JULIETTE continued: *To have sex. I don't see why I should be ashamed of being a woman. Or else, yes there are times when I should feel ashamed to be happy or else just indifferent. Yes, I'm ashamed of that sometimes.* She goes back to the mirror over the washbasin and starts to put on lipstick. *Well, it can't be helped, he's going to put his penis between my legs. I feel the weight of my arm when I move it. Perhaps I should stay with Robert. He doesn't try to get ahead in life. Always satisfied with what he's got. He was just like that in Martinique.*
YOUNG MAN off: *Why are you putting on lipstick?*
JULIETTE: *None of your business!*
Close-up of the young man, a cigarette between his lips, sitting on the bed. His face is covered with freckles. JULIETTE walks past him. He lights his cigarette. JULIETTE's hand

141

appears on screen and strokes the young man's face.

JULIETTE off: *What do you like best?*

YOUNG MAN: *I don't know.*

JULIETTE off: *Do you want to do it the Italian way?*

YOUNG MAN: *What's that?*

JULIETTE off: *You stand and I kneel. That way you can look at me.*
   Insert of a red pane of glass with the word written on it
   back to front.

YTUAEB

YOUNG MAN off: *Yes.*

JULIETTE still off, during insert: *I think it would be nice to be independent sexually. Yet I hate the idea, basically.* Dim close-up of her face as she looks into the camera. *No, humility isn't good really. Yes, there's something so sad about it. Yes, and I'd say the same thing about shame* . . . she lights a cigarette . . . *if it could stop people quarrelling, because it puts a check on everyone's actions according to whether those actions are considered blameworthy or praiseworthy. Other people's blame. Yes, that's also sad, and then it's a bad thing. Yes, like self-contempt and all those feelings.*

YOUNG MAN off: *Will you do it like this?*
   She looks over in his direction.

JULIETTE: *No. Out of the question.*
   Cut to a construction site, showing a vast crane outlined against
   the blue sky. Loud noise of building.
   Close-up of a woman in her forties, smoking a cigarette and
   leaning against a wall with a poster on it.

WOMAN to camera: *She made me an offer.* Camera pans to show blocks of flats, then stops on a huge red sign: PRISUNIC. Continued off. *Thirty thousand francs a day to work in the Madeleine area. I don't think you realize* . . . camera returns to her . . . *I'm a secretary.* Block of flats. Continued off. *I can speak English and Italian. And I can't manage to find a job because I'm too old.* Quick shot of her, then long shot of the blocks of flats with the big petrol station sign: AZUR in the foreground. Continued off. *Yesterday, they told me again at Publicis that they had found nothing for me.*
   Quick shot of the woman. Long shot of a building site, a large
   red lorry empties its load.

TITLE black on red pane of glass, seen in mirror:

COMMENTARY off: *What is art? Someone once said it was that moment in which shapes turn into style.* Postcard of the bay of Monte Carlo, then postcard of the lake at Annecy. *Actually, man himself is style. Thus art is that process whereby shapes become human.*

A beauty parlour. We see a hand holding a small hand-shower against a woman's long hair.

JULIETTE off: *I look at the wall, at various objects. Now . . . never . . . there . . . right now I'm looking out of a window.*

The corner of the beauty parlour. JULIETTE is having her hair washed by one young woman while a manicurist, MARIANNE, does her nails. MARIANNE is a friend of JULIETTE.

MARIANNE: *Hey, you've got a super suntan. Where did you go?*

JULIETTE: *To Russia.*

MARIANNE: *Where?*

JULIETTE: *Silence! To Leningrad.*

MARIANNE: *Are the Russians nice?*

JULIETTE: *Happiness. Oh, they're like anyone else.*

MARIANNE: *I was just asking . . .*

JULIETTE: *But they are rather nice. A few sounds.*

MARIANNE: *By the way, have you seen the Duperrets lately?*

JULIETTE: *Yes, I saw them when I went past the Gare Saint-Lazare.* Pause. *Besides, the truth is that people never know one another.*

MARIANNE: *It's broken.*

JULIETTE speaking to herself: *Robert . . . Christophe.* Pause. *Blue spiral notebooks.*

MARIANNE: *How are you getting on?*

JULIETTE: *Fine.* To herself. *Not to have to make love!*

MARIANNE: *Well, I'd rather do that than work in a factory.*

JULIETTE: *I wouldn't like working in a factory either.*

MARIANNE: *What about your kids? How are they?*

JULIETTE: *They're fine.* Aloud to herself. *What I say with words is never what I'm really saying. They're fine, but very naughty you know.* Voice off. *I'm waiting. . . . I'm watching.*

MARIANNE showing JULIETTE some red nail-varnish: *I'll use this one.*

JULIETTE: *Yes, that'll do.* Voice off. *My hair.* The telephone rings. *The telephone.*

In the foreground of the beauty parlour, a young man sets a customer's hair. The phone goes on ringing, then stops.

MANAGERESS off: *Hello? Yes . . . calling out . . . Marianne! It's for you!*

MARIANNE: *Coming.* She goes up to the cash desk and picks up the receiver. *Hello! Yes. . . . Oh yes . . . yes . . . yes. . . . Hum, hum. . . . Yes . . . yes. . . . Okay. . . . Okay. . .* , She hangs up and calls out as she walks away. *Isn't Yvonne here yet?*

The manageress and Paulette are in the background.

PAULETTE: *No she's not. She's ill.*

MARIANNE stops, then walks back towards a man who seems to be the manager. The phone rings again, off.

MARIANNE: *Mr. Michel! Mr. Michel!*

MICHEL: *Yes?*

MARIANNE: *Do you mind if I leave half an hour early again tonight?*

MICHEL: *Well, you'll have to see about that with Paulette.*

Mr. MICHEL shrugs as MARIANNE walks out of shot towards PAULETTE who is standing in the back.

MARIANNE: *Listen . . . Paulette.*

PAPLETTE: *Yes?*

We see a woman, in profile, sitting under the hair-dryer. She is smoking. On a washbasin in front of her, an advertisement for MOLITG beauty products.

MARIANNE off: *Can you take my place?*

WOMAN CUSTOMER: *I'm ever so careful when I cross the street. You never know when an accident will happen. And then you're finished. . . . Unemployment . . . illness . . . old age . . . death? Never. . . . I don't make any plans about the future, for the future's a dead end.*

PAULETTE at first off. She speaks with a French-Algerian accent: *My name is Paulette Cadjaris.* MARIANNE and JULIETTE are leaving the beauty parlour together. To the camera. *I failed my secretarial course.* Pause. *No, I don't believe in the future. I go for walks. I hate feeling cooped up. I read when I get the chance. Yes, I really enjoy learning about people's characters. I like walking . . . climbing . . . riding a bicycle from time to time. I go to the movies two or three times a month. But not in summer, . . . the theatre? I've never been, but I'd like to go very much. I enjoy reading most. Biographies. Learning about people's lives . . . their personalities,*

144

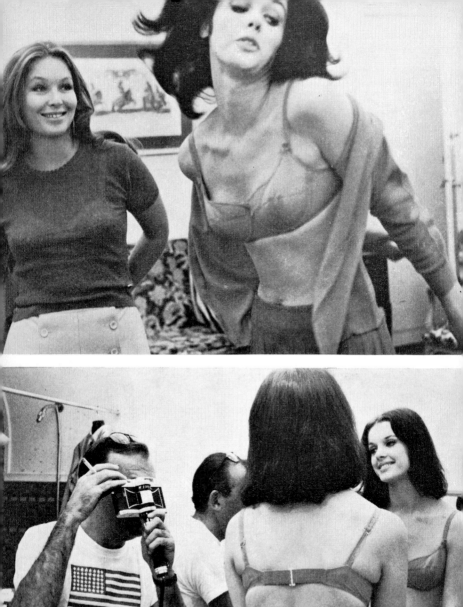

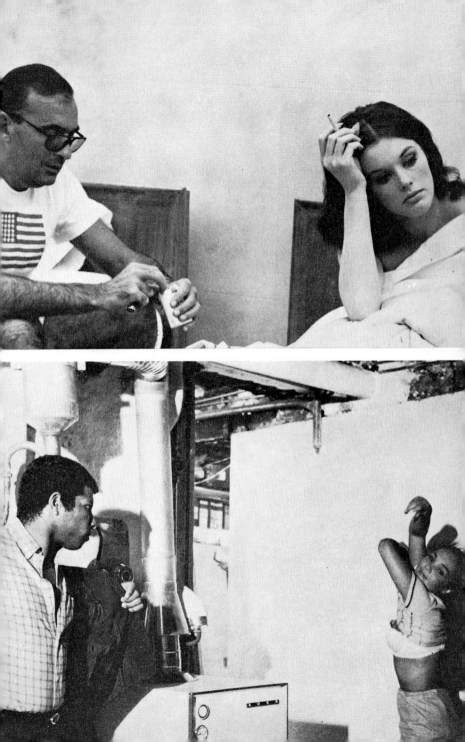

their work . . . travel books, ancient history. A tree. Later, when I marry Francois . . . pause. . . . What else have I done? Nothing very exciting.

She smiles.

Music, then loud construction noises from the building site, where more blocks of flats are being put up.

COMMENTARY off: *Words and images intermingle constantly.*

An avenue on a sunny day. There is a garage with a sign which reads:

CARS PURCHASED

COMMENTARY off: *You can almost say that living in today's world is rather like living in the middle of a big comic strip.* The garage entrance, seen from the street. A bright red Austin 850 drives into the garage. *Yet language alone is inadequate when it comes to describing an image exactly. For example . . .*

ROBERT, his head low down in the frame, walking past an advertisement on the walls of the garage which reads: Mobil Protects. The Austin comes to a stop. MARIANNE and JULIETTE get out. Close-up of an Ariane car with a damaged wing. Behind the Ariane, another sign which reads: 'Operation holiday-check up guarantees pleasant, inexpensive, accident-free travel.' During this last shot the commentary starts again.

COMMENTARY off: *. . . for example, how can you describe an event? What way do you show or explain how, that afternoon, at about ten past four, Juliette and Marianne went to a garage near the Porte des Ternes where Juliette's husband worked?*

ROBERT walks past the car.

JULIETTE gets into the Austin again as one of the garage attendants comes over and shows her where to go. She drives up to the conveyor which will take the car through the automatic wash. She then gets out of the car and joins MARIANNE at the back of the garage. The attendants start working on the car. There is a large yellow arrow painted on the ground, pointing right and left. A man's feet walk across the arrow, going from left to right.

COMMENTARY off: *Sense and nonsense.*

153

Resume on JULIETTE sitting in the Austin which is now next to the petrol pumps. An attendant is filling the tank.

COMMENTARY off: *Yes, how do you describe exactly what happened? Of course, there's Juliette, there's her husband, there's the garage.*

JULIETTE's husband, ROBERT, wearing a blue overall-shirt, goes up to the car and bends down to speak to his wife through the car window. After a brief exchange, he looks at his watch and kisses JULIETTE.

COMMENTARY off: *But do you really have to use those very words and those images? Are they the only possible ones? Are there no others? Am I talking too loud? Am I looking too close or from too far away?*

The husband moves away during the last few words.

TITLE red, white and blue garage sign:

FRICTION
PROOFING

Sound of hooting, off.

The Avenue again. The Austin comes towards the camera and pulls in at the garage.

Close-up of the leaves on the trees which line the street. Zoom back to show the garage sign:

MOBIL

COMMENTARY off: *For example, we have some leaves and even if Juliette doesn't have much in common with a Faulkner heroine, our leaves could be made just as dramatic as those of wild palm trees.*

Head and shoulder shot of a young woman with fair hair (Isabelle Pons) standing in front of the garage wall. Behind her, advertisements for KLEBER-COLOMBES, EYQUEM spark-plugs and DUNLOP.

COMMENTARY continued off: *There's another young woman there too and we don't know a thing about her. We don't even know how to state this fact in the most honest possible way.*

Resume on the garage entrance. An attendant stands next to the large sign:

CARS PURCHASED

154

COMMENTARY continued off: *There's a cloudy sky too if I turn my head and don't just look straight in front of me without moving. And there are some graffiti on the wall.*

The Austin pulls up on front of the garage as it has already done twice before. Return to shot of the Austin coming down the street towards the camera and going into the garage, loudly honking its horn.

TITLE:

CAR
ENTREE

Zoom back so that the sign now reads:

R CAR W
ENTREE ENT

COMMENTARY off: *Why are there so many signs everywhere so that I end up wondering what language is about, signs with so many different meanings, that reality becomes obscure when it should stand out clearly from what is imaginary?*

Zoom forwards so that the sign once again reads:

CAR

In the garage, the Austin is being washed and polished busily by attendants. Roar of car engines being tested, off.

COMMENTARY off: *Images can get away with everything, for better or worse. Ordinary common sense reasserts itself before my very eyes and comes to the rescue of my shattered sense of logic.* Close-up of JULIETTE. *Objects are there, and if I study them more carefully than people it's because they are more real than people.*

Close-up of MARIANNE smoking.

Two garage attendants polishing the Austin. Roar of car engines being tested. Close-up of JULIETTE.

COMMENTARY off: *Dead objects are always alive. Live people are often already dead.*

155

The Austin, facing the camera, slides slowly towards us on the conveyor belt. The noise dies down.

COMMENTARY off: *I'm only looking for reasons to be happy . . . and if I now try to analyse it further, I discover that memory is our chief reason for living, if we have one, and secondly the present and the capacity to live in the present and to enjoy it, finding a reason to live, however fleeting, and enjoying it the space of a few seconds, just as one found it, in its own unique set of circumstances.*

During this commentary, long shot of the garage with its huge MOBIL sign against the blue sky. Then resume on previous shot of JULIETTE inside her car, next to the petrol pumps. ROBERT appears, bends down, talks to her, looks at his watch, kisses her and stands up again. He goes off. We now see JULIETTE from within the car, and through the window, ROBERT walking away. He turns and waves to her.

Outside again. We see MARIANNE's elbow resting on the open car window; the car has been washed and polished so that it gleams in the sun.

COMMENTARY off: *My aim, for the simplest things to come into being in the world of humans, for man's spirit to possess them, a new world where men and things would interrelate harmoniously.* Blurred close-up of leaves reflecting in the red car. *It's really more of a political issue than a poetic one. In any case, it accounts for this passion for self-expression. Whose? . . . Mine. Writer and painter.*

The petrol pump. The indicator rises from 13.20 francs to 16.45 francs.

COMMENTARY off: *It is 16 hours, 45. Should I have described Juliette on the leaves? It was really impossible anyway to describe both . . . so let us just say that the leaves and Juliette fluttered gently in that late October afternoon.*

Resume on the green leaves with the MOBIL sign nearby. Zoom forward to frame leaves in close-up.

Music.

The Champs Elysées. The Arc de Triomphe in the distance. In the foreground, a taxi-rank. A young woman gets into one of the taxis. A man goes up to her and begins talking to her. The young woman gets out of the taxi, the young man slams the taxi door and they walk off together, arm in arm. It is the young man with glasses who spoke to JULIETTE in a previous scene.

The construction site. Blocks of flats being built, there are two concrete mixers.

TITLE:

LE GRAND ESPOIR
DU XXe SIECLE

The building site. A yellow bulldozer is in the foreground.

A courtyard in a housing-estate seen from behind a grille-enclosed bay-window.

INTERVIEWER off: *How long have you been here?*

BOY off: *Me? Three years.*

INTERVIEWER off: *Where are you from?*

BOY off: *Algeria.*

INTERVIEWER off: *Do you like it better here than in Algeria?*

BOY off: *Oh no!*

Two coloured photographs in front of some bushes. Each one shows a couple embracing.

INTERVIEWER off: *Have you got any brothers or sisters?*

BOY off: *I've got a brother and a sister.*

INTERVIEWER off: *What about your parents?*

BOY off: *They're at home.*

INTERVIEWER off: *What does your father do?*

TITLE:

IDEES

BOY off: *He works for an airline.*

INTERVIEWER off: *And your mother?*

BOY off: *My mother . . . she's . . . she doesn't work.*

During the opening of the following commentary, close-up of a key-ring (the kind sold in Pigalle) showing a buxom girl lying down. She is wearing trousers but is naked from the waist up. When the key-ring is tilted slightly, her trousers fall to her ankles and a black bra covers her breasts.

COMMENTARY off: *We have here a meeting of three cultures, the culture of leisure, the key-ring culture, and the culture of Sex. A* street at night. A neon shop sign advertises, in large letters, the

157

word: DRUGS. *And if you don't have enough money to pay for L.S.D., then buy yourself a colour television set.*

The Prince De Galles Hotel. The lift door opens and JULIETTE and MARIANNE emerge, onto the luxurious hotel landing. The lift attendant points to a door and MARIANNE walks forward.

MARIANNE: *It's this one.*

MARIANNE walks beyond the door to a mirror where she hastily runs a comb through her hair. JULIETTE, in the foreground, remains silent.

MARIANNE casually: *Well, what did you expect? Didn't you realize?*

A young groom walks past them.

JULIETTE: *Well, no. . . . I thought it would be fifteen thousand, for the whole night.*

MARIANNE looking shocked as she comes back towards her friend: *What? Fifteen thousand, for a whole night? You must be crazy!*

They walk to the door.

JULIETTE pushing the door: *Shall I go in? It's open.*

They go in. Music. Sound of a door slamming, off.

MARIANNE off: *Yes, sure.*

The Place de la Concorde, looking out towards the construction site near the bridge, where the new underpass is being built.

MARIANNE off: *Oh dear! He's not here.*

MARIANNE and JULIETTE have walked into the suite, closing the door behind them.

JULIETTE gazes at the showy and luxuriously modern decor. MARIANNE wanders from one room to the next, coming back into the main room by a different door each time.

JULIETTE to herself: *I was thinking of this and that. I don't know how it entered my head.* To MARIANNE. *Isn't it huge here?*

MARIANNE: *Yes it is.*

JULIETTE suddenly comes back into the room from a different door. MARIANNE goes past JULIETTE.

JULIETTE astonished off: *Oh! It's got two bathrooms!*

MARIANNE still looking around: *Oh! Oh! Johnny! Johnny!*

JULIETTE comes in as MARIANNE goes out. JULIETTE looks thoughtful as she walks about the room.

MARIANNE off: *Johnny!*

JULIETTE: *Thought either adjusts itself to reality or makes us question it.* Pause. *Question it . . .* MARIANNE joins her . . . *but where is that fellow of yours?*

    Sound of a door opening.

MARIANNE smiling at someone off screen: *Hello!*

AN AMERICAN in English, off: *Hello, Marianne. That's your girl-friend?*

    JULIETTE watches as MARIANNE goes towards the AMERICAN. We hear them kissing.

MARIANNE off: *It is Juliette.*

    JULIETTE moves towards the left, holding an unlit cigarette.

THE AMERICAN off: *Hello.*

JULIETTE: *Hello.*

    The AMERICAN appears, his back to the camera. He is wearing a black and white striped dressing-gown. He picks up a lighter from a table and lights JULIETTE's cigarette. MARIANNE comes into shot and the AMERICAN immediately gives her some money. (*Still*)

THE AMERICAN in English: *Marianne, take a little present for you and undress yourself. Make yourself comfortable.*

    MARIANNE throws down her coat while the AMERICAN takes off his dressing-gown. Underneath, he wears a T shirt with a small US flag sewn on the chest. He goes off screen and the camera remains on the two women.

JULIETTE: *What did he say?*

MARIANNE showing her the money: *We get undressed here.*

    JULIETTE picks up her VOG parcel and takes out the dress she has just bought.

JULIETTE: *I'll wear it when we leave.*

MARIANNE: *Where did you buy it?*

JULIETTE: *At Vog.*

    MARIANNE looks at the dress while JULIETTE puts her share of the money into her handbag.

MARIANNE admiring the dress: *Not bad!* Pause. *Have you seen the Paco Rabane dresses?*

JULIETTE taking off her raincoat: *No. What are they like?*

MARIANNE taking off her blouse: *They're really funny. The dresses are completely made out of little coloured metal scales.*

    She laughs. (*Still*)

    MARIANNE now wearing only her bra, leaves shot.

JULIETTE: *I see!*

MARIANNE: *It's great fun, for parties, of course.*

MARIANNE off-screen throws JULIETTE her blouse.

JULIETTE catches it and drapes it over a chair.

She then starts undoing her skirt.

The AMERICAN faces the camera, holding an eight millimetre movie camera.

MARIANNE crosses the screen, walking towards the bathroom.

THE AMERICAN in English: *My name is John Bogus. I am a war correspondent in Saigon for the Arkansas Daily. I got fed up with the atrocities, with all the bloodshed. So I came here to get some fresh air!*

Still holding the camera, he goes to the bathroom.

MARIANNE stands with her back turned to us, washing her hands. In the mirror, we can see the AMERICAN filming her. (*Still*)

THE AMERICAN in French: *I could say it in French.* MARIANNE holds out her wet hands to him so that he puts down his movie camera to give her a towel; he then picks up a still camera, a Honeywell. *They're stupid and crazy out there. It costs the American Treasury a million dollars to kill one Vietcong. President Johnson could buy twenty thousand girls like these two for the same price.*

He photographs MARIANNE as she combs her hair.

MARIANNE talking to herself: *I existed, that was all I knew. I couldn't have said anything else.*

She turns towards the camera, then goes off screen.

The AMERICAN continues to take photographs while JULIETTE comes on screen and goes over to the washbasin. He takes some photographs of her, then, without saying anything, he puts down his camera, puts on a pair of tinted glasses, gently strokes JULIETTE's hair and goes off-screen.

THE AMERICAN in English off: *Would you like a cigarette?*

In the bedroom. The AMERICAN sits near the bed where MARIANNE, in the foreground, lies under the sheets, her shoulders bare, reading *A Cure for Melancholy* by Bradbury.

MARIANNE in English: *Yes.*

He puts two cigarettes to his lips, lights them and gives one to MARIANNE. (*Still*)

MARIANNE in French: *Is that an ' America uber alles ' T shirt?*

THE AMERICAN in English: *Yes, but it's they who invented the jeep and the napalm.*

He gives her a light, then opens two air-travel bags, a red one and a blue one.

MARIANNE: *Yes, the city is a construction in space, the mobile elements of a city, I don't know. The inhabitants, yes, the mobile elements are as important as the static elements.* Close-up of JULIETTE next to the window, her back to the light; off. *And even the day-to-day, ordinary events in the life of the city can be agreeable in a very special way.*

JULIETTE still standing with her back to the light and talking to herself as she slowly takes off her sweater: *No, an event never occurs in a vacuum. You'll always find that it's related to the circumstances which surround it. Perhaps, quite simply, I am an onlooker. Every city-dweller has his own contacts with specific parts of the city. And with what? Ah! Yes. The image is permeated with meanings and memories. The physical clarity . . .* she switches on a lamp next to her *. . . of this image.* She switches off the lamp. *Paris is a mysterious city.* She turns on the light *. . .stifling . . .* she turns it off *. . . natural.*

She turns the light on then off again.

THE AMERICAN in English off: *Why does she not come over?*

MARIANNE off: *Are you coming, Juliette?*

THE AMERICAN in English off: *Give her one too.*

JULIETTE turning to look at them: *What's going on? Is he crazy?*
Camera follows JULIETTE at shoulder level as she goes over to MARIANNE, who is standing with a red TWA travel bag over her head. MARIANNE gives JULIETTE a blue PANAM bag.

MARIANNE: *Here. He likes it better if we don't see him.*

THE AMERICAN in English off: *Okay, girls. You could start walking now.*

JULIETTE has put the bag over her head and the two women start walking up and down in opposite directions, meeting under a framed landscape.

THE AMERICAN in English off: *Marianne, you could stop now . . .*
Outside. The huge construction site with cranes being operated in front of a building which is near completion.

THE AMERICAN in English off: *Turn around. No, show me your back.*
Pause. *Come this way, Marianne.*

Resume on the two women with the travel bags still over their heads. MARIANNE leaves shot, followed by JULIETTE.

THE AMERICAN in English off: *You could take it off now. And you could tell your girlfriend she can take it off also.*

JULIETTE comes back into shot and stops in the middle of the screen.

MARIANNE off: *You can take it off now.*

JULIETTE takes the bag off her head, stares into the camera then lowers her eyes.

THE AMERICAN in English off: *Will you join us, Juliette?*

MARIANNE off: *Come on, Juliette.*

JULIETTE looking towards them: *No, not that.*

She looks away.

MARIANNE off: *Never mind. I'll do it.*

Insert. Still photographs of wounded Vietcongs taken prisoner by the Americans.

THE AMERICAN in English off: *She got nothing more to say.*

JULIETTE off: *It's strange how a person* . . . resume on close-up of JULIETTE looking at the couple off-screen . . . *living in Europe, on August 17, 1966, can be thinking about another person out in Asia* . . . she lowers her eyes. *To think, to mean to say, that's not the same as writing, running or eating. No.*

Insert. Close-up of the cover of Life magazine. We see a black and white photograph of a wounded American soldier with the caption: WAR GOES ON. Resume on JULIETTE.

JULIETTE: *No, it's an internal process.* She hums a tune and whispers. *If someone asks me to go on singing this song. Well I could, I could go on.* Pause. *What goes into that process? That knowledge that I can go on doing something? I don't know.*

Insert. Close-up, in colour, of a young Vietcong's bloodstained face.

JULIETTE off: *For example, I can think of someone who isn't here. I can imagine him, or else I can bring up the subject all of a sudden.*

Resume on JULIETTE, a thoughtful look on her face.

JULIETTE: *Even if he's dead. For example, I declare* . . . she looks at the couple off-screen . . . *I'm hot* . . . *no, it's just that I'm impatient.*

MARIANNE off: ' *America uber alles!* '

Insert. Close-up of a French, Paris-Match style magazine, black and white photographs of the war in Vietnam with loud noise of machine-gun fire, off. More pages in the same issue, showing photographs of war refugees with caption: 'Van Tuon. . . . These are the survivors. Four hundred tons of bombs have wiped out their villages.' Sound of guns firing and, during JULIETTE's monologue, off, more war photographs.

JULIETTE off: *Now I understand how thought works.*

MARIANNE off: *'America uber alles!'*

Close-up of JULIETTE.

JULIETTE: *It's a matter of replacing the personal observation of reality with an effort of imagination. To say something. . . . To want to say something.* She looks at the couple off-screen. *Yes, it may well be a muscular or a nervous reflex.* Music. *For example, when I say. . . .* End of music. *. . . . I'll go and fetch Robert at the Elysées-Marbeuf café, well now, I'll try to think it without using words, aloud or to myself.*

The last words are spoken off, on the following shot.

Inside the Elysées-Marbeuf café, daytime.

In the background, behind the bar, we see a barman polishing glasses. In front of the bar, a woman is playing the pin-ball machine and we hear the machine rattling throughout the following scene. In the foreground, to the right, ROBERT sits at a table, writing. To the left, one table away, a young girl sits, facing the camera.

FIRST GIRL: *Are you waiting for someone?*

ROBERT still writing: *Yes, for my wife.* The GIRL makes a face, ROBERT scribbles busily: *What about you?*

FIRST GIRL not looking at him: *I'm waiting for someone, but I'm not sure he'll come.* She drinks. *Are you writing to her?*

ROBERT: *No. It's for myself.*

FIRST GIRL taking a cigarette: *Have you got a light?*

ROBERT leans forward to light her cigarette. *Thank you.* A long silence as she smokes. *Pity it's raining.*

The WRITER and the SECOND GIRL come into the café.

BOUVARD off: *Fortunately, things turned out otherwise under Comrade Lenin.*

Cut to two young men facing camera. They are sitting behind a table which is covered with books of every kind. On the wall behind them, a beer advertisement. The two men, who both seem very busy, are called Bouvard and Pecuchet.[1] Bouvard picks up one book after another and reads out a few lines while Pecuchet writes it down. The books are in French, English and Italian, and include fiction, history, guidebooks, telephone directories, etc.

BOUVARD reading aloud: '*Caoutchouc Rigenerato siotienne il caoutchouc rigenerato faciendo speciali tratamenti agli objecti di caoutchouc.*' He picks up another book while Pecuchet goes on writing what is being read out: '*Leon Pelli, moving vans, transport and excursion facilities, 108 rue Joubert-Philips, near the cemetery. Telephone number 295.*' From another book. '*Any man, any time, anywhere, Claudel and . . . got into the yellow . . . while Jessie was running across the yard . . .*' From another book chosen at random like the others. '*The spring water flows solemn, like a dog's mouth. . . . The rose makes me feel shy, she never laughs.*' From another book. '*Purify thyself, Stranger.*' '*I will purify myself before entering,*' Demetrios replied. '*With the wet strands of her hair, the young guardian of the gate moistened his lips, his eyelids and his fingers.*' From another book, '*the scenery in the department of the Hautes Pyrenées, in the heart of the most spectacular Pyrenées country, is extremely varied: 24 Rue du Quatre-Septembre, Paris (2e), telephone: 742 21-34.*' From another book. '*I don't know to this day how madmen are to be prevented from indulging in their wildest fantasies.*' Nikita Kruschev.

The FIRST GIRL stares into space as she drinks up her Coca-Cola.

BOUVARD off: '"*In a year or two, I shall go and work in Paris,*" *she said modestly. It was as if Miss Calendar had the ability to make her play-act.*'

ROBERT off: *Have you got anything else to say to me?*

FIRST GIRL to ROBERT who is off-screen: *No, nothing special. What about you?*

ROBERT off: *Me? Would you like me to tell you what I'm doing?*

FIRST GIRL turning towards ROBERT: *You've already told me, you're writing.*

ROBERT off: *Yes. I'm writing. Something very special. I'm taking down messages dictated to me from outer-space.* She smiles rather

---

[1] From the novel by Gustave Flaubert.

ironically. *Yes, I saw a film like that once, where there was a fellow who did that: Orpheus.* She goes on smoking, the noise from the pin-ball machine is deafening. *Repeat what you said earlier about the rain.*

FIRST GIRL: *That I liked the rain.*

ROBERT off: *No, that isn't what you said.*

FIRST GIRL: *You're right, I didn't say that.*

ROBERT off: *You said . . .*

FIRST GIRL: *. . . that the rain made me feel sad.*

ROBERT off: *Don't you think that's a banal thing to say?*

FIRST GIRL: *No, it's not banal because the rain doesn't make everyone feel sad.*

ROBERT off: *Tell me something else you find interesting.* Pause. *Personally, I find it difficult to really say anything in a film. That's what I'd like to do with you.*

FIRST GIRL: *You'd like to have a real talk with me?*

ROBERT off: *Yes, because I don't know you. I really like talking with a stranger.*

FIRST GIRL: *Go ahead and talk.*

ROBERT off: *Do you know what talking means?*

FIRST GIRL: *Talking means saying words.*

ROBERT off: *And what does saying words mean?*

FIRST GIRL: *Saying words means, either talking about silly things or about fine things.*

ROBERT off: *About what, for instance? How could we talk together? I mean . . . really talk with total commitment on both sides.*

FIRST GIRL: *Well, we choose an interesting subject and talk it over, discuss it.*

ROBERT off: *All right. We'll talk about sex then.*

FIRST GIRL: *Sex, always sex.*

> Throughout this scene, the camera holds on medium close-up of the girl. We hear the noise made by the flippers of the pin-ball machine during the entire conversation.

ROBERT off: *Are you scared?*

FIRST GIRL: *Of course not.*

ROBERT off: *Well, I think you are scared.*

FIRST GIRL: *If that's what you want, I'll say I'm scared. Why should I be scared?*

ROBERT off: *Why on earth are people always scared of sex?*

FIRST GIRL: *But I'm not scared of it.*

ROBERT off: *For example, I'm going to ask you to repeat one sentence and I'm sure you'll refuse.*

FIRST GIRL: *Say it.*

ROBERT off: *But do you promise to repeat it?*

FIRST GIRL: *It depends what the sentence it. Whether I like it or not. If it's intelligent or not.*

ROBERT off: *You see, you are scared.*

FIRST GIRL: *No I'm not scared. It's not a question of being scared.*

ROBERT off: *All right. . . . I'll tell you what to say. Between my legs are my genitals. Go on, say it. Repeat after me.*

FIRST GIRL: *This isn't school.*

ROBERT off: *Then say that sentence.*

FIRST GIRL: *Why should I say it? It's ridiculous.*

ROBERT off: *It's as simple as lighting a cigarette.*

FIRST GIRL: *No it isn't. I light a cigarette because mine's gone out or because I feel like having a smoke, but, to say something so obvious just isn't worth it.*

ROBERT off: *But wait a moment. You've got genitals just like you've got eyes and shoulders.*

FIRST GIRL: *Naturally!*

ROBERT off: *Then why can't we mention the subject?*

FIRST GIRL: *Because I don't talk about my eyes or my shoulders. And I don't talk about my genitals either. That's all.*

ROBERT off: *What a shame. You've got very nice eyes.*

FIRST GIRL: *I don't care.*

ROBERT off: *You've got very nice lips too.*

The girl stares at ROBERT, off-screen, without saying anything for a moment.

ROBERT off: *Look, that fellow over there, across from us, isn't he the Nobel Prize winner?*

FIRST GIRL looking towards the newcomer: *Ivanoff? Could be.*

ROBERT off: *It certainly looks just like him.*

We see a young man sitting with a girl student. They are facing each other, so that we see them in profile. Between them, set into the wall, a mini-jukebox. We can see their reflection as well as ROBERT'S and the FIRST GIRL'S in the mirror behind behind them.

166

SECOND GIRL: *What will the Communist morality be like?*

THE WRITER: *I think it will be much the same as today. He writes a dedication in a book.*

SECOND GIRL: *Yes, but what's that?*

THE WRITER: *Looking after one another, working for one's country, loving it, loving the arts, science.*

SECOND GIRL: *Then how will it be different?*

THE WRITER: *Communism will make it easier to explain.*

SECOND GIRL: *Ah yes! Yes, I understand. It's the money. Money is the great evil because, it leads to theft without our even noticing.* The WRITER *closes the book he has just finished dedicating and smiling, gives it to the girl. A waiter comes into shot, bringing a glass of beer and a coke. Can I ask you something?*

THE WRITER: *Yes, go ahead.*

SECOND GIRL: *Must one be completely honest with oneself?*

THE WRITER: *At your age, definitely.*

SECOND GIRL: *And at your age?*

THE WRITER laughing: *At my age? As honest as possible.*

SECOND GIRL: *No . . . no. She drinks. Always.*

THE WRITER: *That's true. We must always be aware and allow ourselves to be intoxicated by life.*

SECOND GIRL: *May I ask you a question?*

THE WRITER off: *Of course.*

SECOND GIRL smoking: *Does poetry shape our lives or is it merely decorative?*

THE WRITER off: *Everything which is decorative shapes our lives.*

SECOND GIRL drinking: *You just spoke of intoxication, did you mean with beer or with vodka?*

THE WRITER off: *With neither. Without anything.*

SECOND GIRL: *I've never tried either. What is the intoxication of life?*

THE WRITER off: *I think that you, that you know what it is.*

SECOND GIRL: *Me? Oh no. No. She laughs. I'm often depressed you know. I cry an awful lot. Have you got the time to speak to me for a moment?*

THE WRITER off: *Yes, I have.*

SECOND GIRL: *Mind you, I ought to write it down. Oh, but if I wrote it down it would be even harder than like this. Pause. Could you*

167

stop looking at me because I'm ashamed of what I'm about to tell you, but I've got to say it. You're the only one who can help me.

THE WRITER off: *Why me?*

SECOND GIRL: *I don't know.*

> Profile of the WRITER lighting his pipe. He is reflected in the mirror behind him.

THE WRITER: *Why me?*

SECOND GIRL off: *I don't know.*

THE WRITER: *You've got friends, teachers and parents, haven't you?*

SECOND GIRL off: *Yes, I have.*

THE WRITER: *They're not bad people.*

SECOND GIRL off: *No, some of them are nice.*

THE WRITER: *And intelligent?*

SECOND GIRL off: *Yes, intelligent.*

THE WRITER: *Then why me? Have you read my books?*

SECOND GIRL off: *We've studied them at school, but I haven't really read them.*

THE WRITER: *Then don't you think it's odd that you should want to talk to me specifically?*

SECOND GIRL: *I thought you would have more courage.*

THE WRITER off: *It's probably not a matter of courage so much as one of . . .* she drinks *. . . competence.*

SECOND GIRL: *Well then, it would be better if I wrote it down. I should be going now.*

> She smiles shyly and turns her head towards the left.

> Resume on ROBERT still sitting at his table.

FIRST GIRL off: *What about you? If you're so smart, what have you been doing all day?*

ROBERT: *I went to work this morning.*

FIRST GIRL off: *Where?*

ROBERT: *To my garage.*

FIRST GIRL off: *Do you own it?*

ROBERT: *No I don't.* He looks at her.

FIRST GIRL off: *Then why did you say ' my '?*

ROBERT: *You're right. To the garage.*

> On the notebook, on which ROBERT has been writing: ' I am . . . they did not find me . . . too late . . . 5 P mi Bertrand. Clever Bertrand. I come too . . . calm orphan Gaspard. Or I came Bertrand. Calm Orphan. Gaspard from the night.' The red felt-

tip pen crosses out the word ' came '.

FIRST GIRL off: *No, but you're not listening to what I'm saying.*

ROBERT: *Yes I am.*

FIRST GIRL off: *No you're not.* Pause. *How do you know it's a garage? Are you sure you didn't get the name wrong and that it's not a swimming pool or a hotel?*

ROBERT: *Oh! Well, maybe . . . yes. Yes, it could also have a different name.*

As he finishes saying this, the camera returns to the page from the notebook as the felt-tip pen crosses out the word ' calm '.

FIRST GIRL off: *Right, exactly. What accounts for the fact that things have a specific name?*

ROBERT off: *Because we give it to them.*

FIRST GIRL off: *And who gives it to them? You think you know everything, but do you even know yourself?*

ROBERT: *No, not very well?*

BOUVARD off: ' *Gilbert's expression had grown somewhat tense. Martine noticed this and blushed.*' Resume on BOUVARD and PECUCHET still sitting behind a pile of books. ' *Whereas the Hungarian success, which bore the stamp of dualism, was an internal event, the birth of Italy and Germany concerned Europe, particularly Napoleon III.*'

While BOUVARD is reading, the barman comes into shot, his back to us, carrying a tray. He gives MR. PECUCHET a plate of sausages and chips and MR. BOUVARD an egg mayonnaise. He remains there for a moment, then leaves.

BARMAN off: *What'll you have after the egg mayonnaise, Mr. Bouvard?*

BOUVARD off: *Another egg mayonnaise, then some chocolate mousse.* Reading. ' *The fingers of both my hands began to tremble uncontrollably, " now he's going to talk," a voice said. The water stopped flowing and they took the gag off. I could breathe. In the darkness, I could see the lieutenants and the captains with cigarettes between their lips, hitting me hard in the belly to make me throw up the water.*' From another book. ' *Yet thought is not merely questioning and research into non-thought.*'

PECUCHET eats his chips while BOUVARD reads aloud.

BARMAN off: *And what will you have after the hard-boiled eggs, Mr. Pecuchet?*

PECUCHET: *I'd like some ice-cream.*[1]
BOUVARD still reading off: *' Thought is, in its essence,'*
BARMAN off: *We haven't got any ice-cream.*

PECUCHET turns startled; he turns to look at BOUVARD then towards the camera.

BOUVARD reading off: *' vindicated by aid. Thought, as thought, is linked up with the very birth of being. Being to the extent that it is birth. Already, being is destined to thought. Being is, as far as the destiny of thought is concerned.'*

TITLE:

SOCIOLOGIE
DU ROMAN

BLACK WOMAN off: *Are you coming or aren't you?*

In an ill-lit basement, a young black woman is seen walking past an oil-fired boiler.

BLACK WOMAN: *I haven't got all day, you know. Hurry up.*

She goes off to put her coat down somewhere, comes back, takes off her sweater (*Still*) and leaves again.

A young sturdy-looking black man comes into shot, walks over to another door then comes back towards the woman.

BLACK MAN: *Why not in there?*

The man takes off his jacket, while the woman speaks off.

BLACK WOMAN off: *Can't you see there's no room left!*

He walks towards her and out of shot.

A road on a sunny day. A red car drives past a modern-looking petrol station and then stops. Sound of a lorry engine. A road leading to the housing-estate. A huge, double-deck car transporter, carrying Simcas 1500, goes past, followed by the Austin. JULIETTE and her husband sit inside the car. JULIETTE turns down a side road leading to the housing-estate. Resume on the highway. A huge goods lorry with the name R. Ollivier painted on its tarpaulin cover, thunders past, followed by JULIETTE's Austin. As in the previous shot she turns down a side road.

---

[1] Pecuchet, in fact asks for a *mystère,* which is a kind of ice-cream and a pun on the word mystery. Translator's note.

170

COMMENTARY off: *You no longer need fortuitous events to photo-graph and to kill the world.*

Inside the Prisunic.

A cashier facing camera. She picks up one item after another as it rolls past her on the conveyor belt and taps out the price of each purchase on her cash register.

The housing-estate. The Austin is in the distance.

TITLE section of a sign:

BAB

COMMENTARY off: *To rediscover the A.B. the A B of life.*

JULIETTE stands in front of a block of flats.

Children's cries, off.

JULIETTE to camera: *Nor when? I only remember that it happened. Perhaps it's not important. It was while I was walking with the fellow who worked in the metro, as he took me to the hotel. It was an odd feeling. I've been thinking about it all day. The feeling of my links with the world.*

She turns her head towards the right and the camera follows her gaze in a vast, circular 360° pan of the blocks of flats all around, during the continuation of her monologue off.

JULIETTE off: *I suddenly had the feeling that I was the world and that the world was me. I'd need a lot of space to describe it. I'd need a whole book and more.* Resume on her face. *The landscape is like a face. One might be tempted to say: All I see is a face wearing a special expression. But . . . pause . . . that doesn't mean that there's anything unusual about the expression, or that one is going to attempt to describe it. Perhaps one feels like saying: it's like this or like that. She looks like Tchekov's Natasha . . . she smiles . . . or else she's like the sister in Flaherty's Nanouk. But it would be more accurate to say: you can't put it into words . . . yet I feel that the expression on my face must mean something . . . something which is outside the general pattern. I mean, the sort of pattern which . . .* the next few words are drowned by the noise of car-horns. *It's as if it were possible to say at first: there's a special expression on this face . . . and then . . . and then . . . actually, it's this one. Tiredness, for instance . . .*

TITLE sign behind the glass door of a shop:

OLD LADY off: *I used to live in the XVI arrondissement. Then they sold our appartment. Now we're stuck here. Not quite the same . . . eh . . . ?*

Large hoarding covered with various advertisements and bill posters, some of them half torn off.

On one small, undamaged poster we read the words:

PEACE IN VIETNAM
WE MUST ACT
WE MUST DEMAND IT

Sound of bombs exploding in an air raid.

At the bottom of the screen, we see ROBERT's head.

He is pacing up and down, obviously waiting for someone.

JULIETTE comes into shot from the right and goes up to her husband while he lights a cigarette.

JULIETTE: *What shall we do?*

ROBERT starts pacing up and down again, stopping to light his cigarette.

ROBERT: *We'll start again.*

JULIETTE crosses over to him, takes his cigarette and walks off. (*Still*)

Cut to a young woman facing camera. Loud cries of children.

CHILDREN BEING INTERVIEWED off: *Ah yes! It's nice here. We have loads of fun.*

TITLE:

IDEES

Housing estate near a garage.

CHILDREN off: *Yeah, we have fun, but there isn't much to do. No. They ought to build a playground. They only have ladders over there, but you can break a leg.* Laughter off.

TITLE:

ON SALE HERE

172

Children looking out of dusty council flat windows.

CHILDREN off: *There used to be a merry-go-round but they took it away. There were some swings, but they've gone. Yeah, we have lots of fun. If only we could find something to do.*

Inside a block of flats. CHRISTOPHE is sitting on the stairs. The lift door on the landing above him opens, but CHRISTOPHE ignores it. He reads a school book, his satchel lies next to him. JULIETTE walks out of the lift, wearing her dress from Vog, followed by ROBERT who carries a paper bag full of groceries. They stop in front of the door to their appartment.

JULIETTE: *Right, you go and fetch the children.*

ROBERT leaving: *Sure . . . sure . . .*

JULIETTE: *What about the key?*

ROBERT: *Sure . . . sure.*

ROBERT leaves. JULIETTE looks down and notices CHRISTOPHE sitting on the stairs.

JULIETTE: *Oh, so you're there? . . . What are you doing?*

She goes over to her son, bends down and gives him a kiss.

CHRISTOPHE: *I'm doing my homework.*

JULIETTE: *What's the subject?*

CHRISTOPHE: *Friendship. I'll read it to you.*

JULIETTE: *Yes.*

CHRISTOPHE reading aloud: '*There are both boys and girls at our new school this year, which means that our class is mixed. Is friendship between boys and girls possible and desirable, yes or no?*'

While CHRISTOPHE reads aloud, JULIETTE takes the small diary out of her handbag, jots something down, puts it away again.

CHRISTOPHE reading: '*Yes, because some of the girls are very nice, very honest. Maryse, Martine, Ghislaine, Roseline. We have nice talks with those girls. "Hello, funny mug," I say to Claudia. She says, "Hello, how are you?"*' He hesitates. '*Then we have a talk until we start to disagree. "Shut up!" he says. "Yes, but you said that to me." "Calm down." In that case, I agree and we go on talking. In this case . . . friendship is desira . . . ble because the girls are nice. With Maryse and Roseline, we have con. . . . We have serious conversations. "Did you find the answer to the problem?" Roseline asked, errr . . . err . . . H. . . .*' JULIETTE bending over and taking the notebook: *Wait. . . .* She turns over the pages. '*H'OB=AOB.*

173

No. A'OB $= \dfrac{AOB}{2}$ *. . .'* She looks up as ROBERT arrives with the whimpering SOLANGE. *All right. . . . To* ROBERT. *As you wish!*

> CHRISTOPHE aims at his mother with a plastic machine-gun while JULIETTE waves to SOLANGE.

JULIETTE reading aloud: *' Friendship in this case is also possible. No, because some other girls are mean and look dishonest . . .'*

ROBERT opening their front door: *Are you coming, Juliette?*

JULIETTE: *Yes . . . , yes. . . . She goes on reading. ' Those who wear glasses. In that case, we do not have peaceful conversations, we argue. " Oh! " she says, " You're horrible." '*

> JULIETTE gets up and gives the notebook back to CHRISTOPHE who takes it and puts down his toy machine-gun.

JULIETTE: *Okay, you go on.*

CHRISTOPHE while she speaks: *Please, Mummy, can I go on?*

JULIETTE going off: *All right.*

CHRISTOPHE reading aloud: *' " Brrrr . . ." she says. " You're horrible." I don't reply but I give her a kick. She throws something in my face and then we stop because the teacher. In this case, friendship is not possible and not desirable. I would rather be on the electric chair with my feet in a glass of water.'* Close-up of CHRISTOPHE, still reading. *' All the same, these mean and nice girls are clean and, on the whole, nice, so I don't mind too much.'*

> He picks up his machine-gun again, aims at the camera and fires twice.
>
> In JULIETTE's kitchen, JULIETTE comes in, followed by ROBERT.

ROBERT: *Ouf. Here we are!*

JULIETTE: *Where?*

ROBERT going off screen: *Home.*

JULIETTE: *And what'll we do after that?*

ROBERT off: *We'll sleep. . . . What's the matter with you?*

JULIETTE: *And after that?*

ROBERT off: *We'll wake up.*

JULIETTE taking out the groceries: *And after that?*

ROBERT off: *The same. All over again.* JULIETTE opens a cupboard and puts a package of Lustucru noodles on the shelf. *We'll work. We'll eat.*

JULIETTE: *And after that?*

ROBERT comes back into shot and stands facing JULIETTE. He takes off his glasses.

ROBERT: *I don't know.* Pause. He looks at his wife and puts on his glasses. *We'll die.*

JULIETTE: *And after that?*

A petrol-pump counter registering from 00.00 to 01.10.

JULIETTE is sitting on a bed. Behind her, CHRISTOPHE sinks down onto the bed; we hear SOLANGE crying and whimpering, off.

CHRISTOPHE: *Please, Mummy, can I play a little, can I read something?*

JULIETTE stroking his hair: *Yes, go ahead.*

CHRISTOPHE jumping on the bed: *Thanks, Mummy!*

He goes on jumping up and down, singing to himself, while JULIETTE looks very thoughtful.

JULIETTE to herself: *What is it, to know something?* Aloud. *Robert, Please bring Solange over here . . .* turning to face the camera. *To show my eyes. I know they're my eyes because I see out of them. I know they're not my knees or anything else because that's what I've been told.* To CHRISTOPHE. *Will you keep still for a moment!*

CHRISTOPHE: *Yes, Mummy.*

JULIETTE to the camera: *How would it be if I hadn't been told? And what about living?* Sound of SOLANGE crying off. *Where's your daddy?*

Music. ROBERT brings the whimpering SOLANGE into the room, carrying her in his arms. CHRISTOPHE has slipped into bed and picked up a book. The father kisses both children and leaves the room. SOLANGE calls out after him:

SOLANGE: *Daddy! Daddy!*

JULIETTE rocking SOLANGE in her arms: *Don't you want to have a nice sleep with Christophe?*

In the living-room. ROBERT with his back to the camera, is operating the radio set. He puts the earphones on, looks at a piece of paper, listens and writes down something. On the right, we can see a corner of the kitchen.

ROBERT: *If Hitler came here, I'd shoot him.* Pause. *How can I say that? Because I'd wait for him.* As he speaks, he waves CHRISTOPHE's plastic machine-gun about and aims it off-screen. *And the moment he comes in, I'll shoot him.* He shoots; sound of real machine-guns.

175

He puts down the toy weapon and turns to face the camera. *No, I don't know where he is, when I don't know, I imagine.* He goes back to his writing. *How was I able to imagine something when I didn't know where it was?* He turns towards the camera again. *No, I don't know if he still exists.* He turns away. *Yes perhaps I'm confusing thought with reality. Yes, yes, I'd be tempted to write that down.* Turning to face the camera again, then writing. *That as there aren't real objects to guarantee the truth.* He faces the camera again. *The truth of our thoughts is not what we think of as reality . . .* JULIETTE comes from the kitchen into the room and walks towards the camera, ROBERT gazes at her . . . *it's the ghost of reality.*

JULIETTE: *What?*

ROBERT staring at her: *Not certain!*

JULIETTE going off: *The children are asleep.*

ROBERT: *Oh, that's good!*

    In ROBERT and JULIETTE's bedroom, night-time.

    JULIETTE sits up in a double bed, facing the camera and wearing blue pyjamas. Music. Above the bed, a film poster.

JULIETTE: *To define oneself in a word: Not yet dead!* She picks up a book from the bed and starts reading from it. '*The man with a future has an above average practical intelligence which includes the capacity to make judgments . . .'*

    ROBERT comes in, sits down on the bed and takes off his shoes, shirt and socks while JULIETTE goes on reading aloud.

JULIETTE continuing to read: '*and an extensive general knowledge. In a survey of two thousand, five hundred and eighty-nine employees, Richardson, Buloz, Henry and Co. discovered that directors and board members scored an average of eighty-four points in intelligence tests. Managers and foremen scored an average of seventy-eight points . . . , while skilled mechanics and unskilled workers scored an average of seventy-four points. The man with a future is self-confident without being aggressive.* Pause. *Was it you who underlined that?*

ROBERT undressing: *Yes.*

JULIETTE still reading aloud: '*The man with a future is ready to admit he has problems and to recognise his faults. Such a man is not afraid to say: "I don't know." One gets the impression that it is only people who have confidence in themselves who can admit an error.'* Pause. *I don't agree with that.*

176

ROBERT takes the book away from her, puts it down on his pillow and goes on undressing.

ROBERT: *If you don't like it, read something else.*

JULIETTE, annoyed, picks up a woman's magazine, Elle, and starts looking through it. ROBERT takes off his trousers and gets into bed, wearing his vest and pants. The couple and the bed are red, white and blue. JULIETTE in blue, ROBERT in white, under the red blanket.

JULIETTE: *Can you tell the difference between real love and the other kind.*

ROBERT: *No, what is it?*

He puts on his glasses, picks up his books and starts to read.

JULIETTE: *'The false kind of love is when I go back to being myself. Real love is when I alter and the other person changes too.'*

ROBERT looking at his book: *Do you think I've changed? I haven't but I'm tired, you know.*

JULIETTE: *No, not you. Me.* Pause. *I've changed and yet I've gone back to being myself, so what does it mean?*

They look at each other.

ROBERT reading: *I don't know.*

JULIETTE: *Well, if you don't know, give me a cigarette.*

He stretches out his arm, takes a packet of cigarettes from the bedside table which is also a stereo loudspeaker. He gives his wife a cigarette which she lights immediately, then he goes back to his reading. (*Still*) Close-up of the match flame and the glowing tip of the cigarette against a black background.

COMMENTARY off: *I listen to the commercials on my transistor radio. . . . Thanks to Esso, I drive safely to the land of my dreams and I forget the rest. I forget Hiroshima, I forget Auschwitz, I forget Budapest, I forget Vietnam, I forget the S.M.I.G., I forget the housing shortage, I forget the famine in India.*

The cigarette seems to go out during the commentary, so that the screen goes black; then it starts to glow again, probably because JULIETTE has just taken another puff. This happens several times, then:

TITLE:

IDEES

Photograph of a couple in an advertisement for Hollywood chewing-gum. Zoom back to reveal a variety of consumer goods set out in such a way as to remind one of great blocks of flats in a housing estate. The ecstatic-looking couple advertising the chewing-gum is surrounded by boxes of Lava, Omo, Dash, Ajax, Schick razor-blades, Lustucru noodles and various brands of cigarettes.

COMMENTARY off: *I've forgotten everything except that, as I'm going back to zero, I'll have to use that as my point of departure.*

Zoom continues, then fade out black; two chords of music and the word FIN appears on screen in red, white and blue letters.

CRITICAL APPENDIX

A Woman is a Woman (1961)

From *A Woman is a Woman* by Edgardo Cozarinsky — first published in *The Films of Jean-Luc Godard* (Studio Vista)

From the broken up, sparkling credits with back stage noises on the sound track, there is a festive excitement about *A Woman is a Woman*. But what is celebrated is not so easy to recognize. Paris? (There is a reference to René Clair's *14 Juillet* in the credits.) A certain approach to the *ménage à trois* comedy? (Belmondo's surname in the film is Lubitsch, and the story line could be read as Lubitsch's *Design for Living* brought up to date.) Anna Karina? (Very evidently.)

But the idealized, intermittently musical daily life of Clair's early talkies is part of a vanished world as is Lubitsch's tenuous web of ellipses which rescued the most banal situations. Godard's Paris and the people who inhabit its noisy boulevards have no real roots, and the quotations in which he delights only bring this out more clearly. In *A Woman is a Woman*, as in his more obviously serious films, it is this uprootedness of modern experience that Godard explores and dramatizes (or exposes by de-dramatizing?). Even this close-knit texture of small bistros, strip-tease joints, political suspicion and conjugal wavering is constantly violated in its naturalistic surface, not just by the comic turns of the plot but by Godard's reminders not only that the film is a performance, but that the projected images are themselves illusory. Karina walks behind a pillar in her strip gear and appears completely dressed in her street clothes. Later she flips into the air the egg she is frying, goes to answer the telephone and comes back to catch the egg in the pan. We are in a world whose Columbus was Méliès.

The film has a beauty that is brash and pathetic, like splintered coloured glass, fragments that somehow compose a picture while refusing to hold together: musical, sad, uproarious, definitely frail. It is this simultaneous celebration of beauty and its frailty, of gaiety and its ephemerality, of the transient nature of all emotion, that reveals in *A Woman is a Woman* a peculiar romantic attitude, reserved and self denying, which is perhaps the only possible romanticism for a contemporary sensibility.

Even the plot devices of low comedy are here emptied of their mechanical utility and turned into the absurd particulars that clutter this day in November 1961, the day when Karina may conceive the child she wants. She uses the little calculating wheel, not to know when she may have intercourse without danger, but to make sure of its consequences — an ironic reversal that invests the little contraption with oracular dignity.

The characters who are called to perform are helpless and confused. Greek mythology, Hölderlin and Fritz Lang, are brought into *Contempt* as dialectical arguments, arousing the characters into attitudes, illuminating their predicament with a moral reflection they cannot achieve by themselves. Film mythology sustains this function almost unaided in *A Woman is a Woman*. There are many familiar traits in both Karina's Angela and Michel Piccoli's Paul in *Contempt*. According to Belmondo, Angela is ' a girl who always makes mistakes '. He draws this moral from his story about the girl who believes she has mixed up the notes written to her two lovers, and loses both by believing in her mistake; Paul makes clumsy efforts to ingratiate himself with his wife and his boss, and only manages to lose everything he cared for. *Contempt* is an almost solemn meditation on the inadequacy of a divided sensibility for dealing with a classical, well defined set of moral issues. ' To explain Paul, one could also say that he is a character from *Marienbad*, who wants to play a character in *Rio Bravo*.' These are Godard's own words in the film's first treatment.

Angela, and in a way also Belmondo's Alfred, feel the same nostalgia for an unattainable, clear territory. They talk about their longing to be Cyd Charisse and Gene Kelly, and immediately appear fixed in impossible postures against their drab, everyday surroundings. These shots are not frozen, for that would suggest an illusion of performance, but the actors themselves try laboriously to hold postures for which they have neither the natural ability nor the professional training, and their quivering arms and legs indicate the effort. Karina will never be Cyd Charisse, nor Belmondo Gene Kelly, just as in *Breathless* he could never be Bogart in spite of his appropriation of the speech mannerisms and lip rubbing. Both are creatures of a precarious world that is conscious of its own precariousness. The hard certainties of the traditional American film are beyond their reach.

Godard incorporates in the film all the dead matter, the opaque, meaningless surfaces of experience, which, like trivia in an assemblage, acquire meaning and exert an active function in their new context. A dialogue between Karina and Marie Dubois is composed of the casual sights they register while walking down the street. *Tu te laisses aller,* Aznavour's song coming from the jukebox in the bistro sequence, is heard complete, its three minutes in the soundtrack filled on the screen by close-ups of a worried Karina inspecting photographs of Brialy and Belmondo with some cheap whores. Another instance of Godard's inclusion of found material, systematically practised in *A Married Woman,* almost to the point of making out of the editing of magazine ads and street signs a kind of *art trouvé,* is the repeated sequence where Karina and Brialy, having decided not to speak to each other, communicate their mutual resentment showing (complete or partially obscured) book titles. This is, of course, a light-hearted game, far from the ominous or ironical weight that street signs have acquired in Godard's later films.

There is even a moment of revelation when Godard edits into the film an unsuccessful take. Karina, in close-up, defends her emotionalism against Brialy's common sense. ' Women who cry are beautiful,' she says. ' I think they're stupid, the modern women who try to litim . . . no . . . that's not right, is it? ' she asks, realizing her mistake, and immediately comes the good take — ' I think they're stupid, the modern women who try to imitate man.' By preserving the anguish of the character together with Karina's distress at her limited French, Godard has removed all distinction between Angela and the actress playing the role. The film has been justly defined as a documentary on Anna Karina, but it is Godard's invariable basic rule to expose the dramatic convention of his film (his debased Brechtianism, as his detractors call it) and make the spectator aware all the time that what he sees are actors illustrating an action for his benefit. In a moment of anger, Karina threatens to go back to Copenhagen; in another Brialy makes fun of her incapacity for rolling the French ' r '; by the end of the film it is she who appears to correct Brialy's pronounciation, only to make one of those puns of which Godard is so fond. ' *Angela, tu es infame,*' he says, after satisfying her wish for maternity, so that they may never know if the possible child is his or Belmondo's, with whom she has been some hours earlier. ' *Non,*' she corrects, ' *je suis* une *femme* ' pretending to have understood *une femme* instead of *infame.*

It is this impossibility of recognizing a definitive meaning in appearances that Godard dramatizes rather than using it to build up an aesthetic system, like Robbe-Grillet. Words may sound alike; faces may look alike; the expression on the face that says a mistaken line may be the right one. Karina was to express her disgust of language (spoken against shots of the back of her neck) in the first sequence of *Live Your Life,* and later in the same film she questioned Brice Parain on the subject. Throughout *Contempt* there is a very involved play of different languages and approximate or deficient translation. These issues are present in *A Woman is a Woman* as obstacles between the characters and their understanding of themselves. Karina asks Belmondo to say a lie (that it's raining) and then to say the truth (that the sun is shining) and can't see any difference in his face. ' There should be one, because a truth is different from a lie.'

The distrust of appearances and the emphazing of dramatic convention account for the film's extensive use of play-within-a-play devices. A quarrel in the kitchen is framed by the open door, and Karina reminds Brialy that they should bow to the audience before beginning to insult each other. Music comes in operatically full-blown rushes after each sentence spoken at the dinner table, underlining the speech as in a recitative. When left alone, Karina enacts a wish fulfillments routine with a pillow under her cardigan, moving in front of the mirror like a pregnant woman would. She also reads very emphatically, and turns out the lights at the end. (Camille is the name of the character in the tirade she reads and also Bardot's name in *Contempt,* both possibly homages to Renoir's *La Carrozza d'Oro,* not only the most perfect and beautiful film made about *la paradoxe du comédien,* but also one of the most influential, from a theoretical point of view, upon French film makers of Godard's generation.)

But, finally, the film's chance of beauty lies in the preservation of Angela's (Karina's) frail emotions and stubborn will, amid the detonations of colour and sound that build up its fun-fair mood.

Between Brialy's shallow practicality and the outsider's romanticism and resignation of Belmondo, the only way she has to realize her wish is the absurd one she chooses. In a world devoid of certainties, the conventions of a vaudeville can work seriously. 'I don't know if I should laugh or cry,' she says, and it is later said of the whole proceedings that it doesn't matter if they are a comedy or a tragedy, being anyway a masterpiece. *A Woman is a Woman* may not be a masterpiece, and I am not even sure if it is a very good film. But somehow I don't care. If standards of judgement must adapt to the changing nature of the judged matter, the only way to come to terms with a the film, as with all of Godard's output, is to appreciate the range of meaning not imprisoned in the work but alluded to, pointed at, juggled with, even contradicted. This is, in a way, a conditional art, self-questioning, investigating the sensibility of the 'sixties on more levels than journalism, the plastic arts or social anthropology have dared to tread.

A Married Woman (1964)

From *Godard on Godard* edited by Jean Narboni and Tom Milne (Secker & Warburg Ltd, 1972)

There are several ways of making films. Like Jean Renoir and Robert Bresson, who makes music. Like Sergei Eisenstein, who paints. Like Stroheim, who wrote sound novels in silent days. Like Alain Resnais, who sculpts. And like Socrates, Rossellini I mean, who creates philosophy. The cinema, in other words, can be everything at once, both judge and litigant.

Misunderstandings often arise from the failure to remember this truth. Renoir, for instance, may be accused of being a bad painter, whereas no one would say this of Mozart. Resnais may be accused of being a bad story-teller, whereas no one would think of saying this of Giacometti. The whole, in other words, is confused with the part, denying either one the right of exclusion as well as inclusion.

This is where the trouble begins. Is the cinema catalogued as a whole or a part? If you make a Western, no psychology; if you make a love story, no chases or fights; if you make a light comedy, no adventures; and if you have adventures, no character analysis.

Woe unto me, then, since I have just made *A Married Woman*, a film where subjects are seen as objects, where pursuits by taxi alternate with ethnological interviews, where the spectacle of life finally mingles with its analysis: a film, in short, where the cinema plays happily, delighted to be only what it is.

From a review in *The Observer*, 11.4.1965, by Kenneth Tynan

' Fragments of a film ' is how Jean-Luc Godard describes *A Married Woman*, his latest bulletin on the crisis of contemporary morals. By this he intends no insolence: the phrase implies not that the film is slapdash or unfinished, but that it faithfully records the fragmented vision of a girl who cannot make the disparate splinters of her life add up to a coherent whole. The twenty-four hours through which we follow her are not a smooth dramatic progression, rising to a climax and then achieving resolution. They are a staccato series of impressions — caresses, rebuffs, insights, stupidities, transient ups and downs — as befits a girl who lives entirely in the present.

Her lover, in whose bed the film starts, is an actor: her husband, once loved and still slept with, is a pilot. Both have normal memories; but for her, each new experience erases what happened a moment ago. Which of the two should she choose? Tousled, puzzled and weakly well-meaning, Macha Meril makes her dilemma universal. In what sound like unscripted interviews, she questions people about the purpose of life. (With small hope of enlightenment, since we already know that words *per se* confuse her: *je suis*, in her mind, suggests the first person singular of *suivre*.)

A middle-aged intellectual advises her to inject a little reason into absurdity, which baffles her utterly. Finding herself pregnant, she quizzes a doctor on birth-control and the relevance of pleasure to love — getting nothing in return but a suave display of fence-sitting. She asks the actor whether he is acting when he makes love to her; but since he may still be acting when he replies, we are left as much in the dark as she is.

What kind of world is it that can set her moral signposts so capriciously spinning? The clue is that she works for a fashion magazine; here is a world of second-hand images. The camera roams over girdle and brassiere ads., zooms in on romantic headlines (so that ' Danger ' becomes ' Ange '), and plasters the screen with record

184

sleeves and movie hoardings. The heroine worries about her posture, snips her pubic hair, and measures the distance between her nipples because magazines tell her to. In a hilarious, dead-pan sequence — we forget how funny Godard can be, with his sleepless eye for banality — her husband describes their flat to a guest in the fulsome terms of an estate agent's brochure.

What Godard wants to show is how ideas and moral concepts are shaped by the very means through which they are received. As Marshall McLuhan has explained in his book, *Understanding Media*, the invention of the printing press created a new sort of human being — the individualist — by making knowledge portable and privately digestible. We are now moving into a new era of continuous assault on all the senses by all the pop media — TV records, films, advertising and journalism. Godard's heroine is living through the transition: hence her moral numbness and sense of impermanence.

According to McLuhan, the mechanised media will take us beyond ' fragmented, literate and visual individualism ' into a deeper, broader, more multi-sensual life. Like most of us, however, Godard at once resents and relishes mass communications; hence his readiness to expose Mlle Meril to their bombardment, and the fascination with which we watch her reactions. The film stings and tickles by turns, and always enlists the mind. As lover and husband respectively, Bernard Noël and Phillipe Leroy are casually perfect.

Two or Three Things I Know About Her (1965)

From *Two or Three Things I Know About Her* by Stig Bjorkman — first published in *The Films of Jean-Luc Godard* (Studio Vista).

In the summer of 1966 Godard was making two films simultaneously, *Made in USA* and *Deux ou trois choses que je sais d'elle*, and the two films have various things in common.

Both *Made in USA* and *Two or Three Things* were inspired by real events. The former drew on certain aspects of the Ben Barka affair to build up a nightmarish picture of a paralyzing political atmosphere, a plot full of real but invisible menace. *Two or Three Things* takes as its point of departure a feature in *Le Nouvel Obser-*

vateur in which the journalist Catharine Vimonet writes of *les étoiles filantes,* that is those housewives in the modern suburbs of Paris who pass the time and make some pin-money as part-time prostitutes. Some points raised by the article, and by some of the readers' letters following it, are the basis for Godard's film with its eighteen lessons about the modern industrial civilization.

Two or Three Things forms a *collage* of opinions and images. The film is as fragmented as *Made in USA* and there is the same verbal disintegration, but in style and content it belongs with Godard's sociologically most ambitious films, *It's my life (Vivre sa vie) A Married Woman, Masculin-Feminin. Two or Three Things* takes the form of a series of confrontations with French everyday life and the people in it. People are caught unawares as they go about their daily tasks. They are interviewed and exchange confidences with the audience, either in shy testimony or open confession

We are often thrown into Godard's films with brutal directness. The 'action' of the film has already begun before we are facing it, as in *A Woman is a Woman,* or *Pierrot le Fou,* or *Made in USA* which opens with a shot of Anna Karina and the words: 'Happiness, for instance . . .'

Two or Three Things commences with four views of modern city life in Paris, whether bursting with the noises of modern construction work or enveloped in total silence as if the image of the city was being laid out for a post-mortem, followed by a shot of Marina Vlady at the window of her suburban flat.

This is succeeded by a shot of the same window, same actress, but seen from another angle: 'She is Juliette Janson. She lives here. She is wearing a sweater with blue stripes. She's got fair hair, or maybe light brown. I'm not sure.'

There we have the image of the actress and the image of the part she is playing. Godard does not make a distinction, and later on in the film when Juliette is speaking she uses the words of Marina Vlady. Still, we must bear in mind the task of the actress to communicate a character which is not her own. She discusses the part, announces her sympathies and the points on which her opinions diverge. Here we have Brecht's theories on the quoting actor.

But the *she* of the film is neither Marina nor Juliette but Paris. Godard shows us a city in a state of change. A new city is being constructed but it doesn't shape itself to the wishes and expectations of the inhabitants. On the contrary, they must adapt their needs to fit the workings of the city. Thus conflicts arise, and also an isolation which Godard portrays more concretely and directly than for instance Antonioni in his tales of modern life.

The main character of the film is a married woman in her thirties. She has two children and she lives in the midst of the harshly urbanised townscape which Godard manages to represent with an equally strong sense of vulgarity and fascination. The day of her life that Godard has chosen to portray is no extraordinary day either for Juliette or for those women who might identify themselves with her situation. 'You go on using gas and water and electricity without giving a thought to the end of the month when the bills will have to be paid. It is always the same. Either it is no money to pay the rent or no telly. Or else we keep the telly, but no car. Or a washing-machine but no holiday. Therefore in no way a normal life.'

Godard puts the blame squarely on those responsible for planning her environment (Paul Delouvrier, prefect and later head of administration, is even mentioned by name). Godard does not hide his radical political views, and he openly accuses the authorities of playing into the hands of big-time capitalism in creating an environment which exercises an economic constraint on the people in it. Godard sees an inhuman milieu emerging in which the inbuilt demand for an ever higher standard of living creates a feeling of menace. Instead of revolting, the workers have adjusted to the bourgeois system and its conditions of capital distribution and acquisitiveness. Through overtime and second job they endeavour to live up to the economic demands that are put on them. They are the victims of an image of society dictated by advertising and they find it difficult to defend themselves against the seductive slogans advertising inessential goods and services. Consider the absurd *déjeuner sur l'herbe*, with all its synthetic goods, which Godard lays out in the film.

Juliette is also the perfect consumer. In her, there is no hesitation between the wish and its fulfilment. She reacts languidly to the impulses she receives from modern advertising techniques. She prostitutes herself to give force to this action. Juliette lives right in the middle of what Godard sees as the comic strip of present-day life and society. There is (according to one of Juliette's customers)

America über Alles — and *pax americaine* is the super-economical (brain-) washing-powder.

Godard is preoccupied with world problems and futilities. Juliette's husband who works in a garage is also a radio ham. He sits at his receiver tuning in to voices and words about far-flung theatres of war, present and future. He has tuned in to the red line between Washington and Saigon; he hears President Johnson ordering an escalation of the war and a stepping-up of the bombings of Hanoi and Haiphong, Peking and Moscow.

One might describe the construction of *Two or Three Things* by likening it to a number of transparent discs differently patterned which have been put on top of one another. Together they form a complete image. Remove one disc, shut your eyes to one aspect of Godard's film, and the pattern will change, however slightly. The film reflects a kind of new realism with quite a few qualities in common with the *nouveau roman*: economy and precision of detail; a vision giving an extraordinary depth of perspective through the sudden switches between close-up and long-shot.

Two or Three Things has a quality which is completely lacking in Godard's earlier work — hesitation. The film has a contemplative feeling and a calm which is unusual. Godard tries to find order in the chaos which he experiences. He says that he wants to define himself with one or two simple words. 'Ensemble' is a word which often occurs in his and Juliette's conversations, but the communion they are looking for seems impossible for them to attain. The film reflects homelessness — social, political and moral.

Godard queries his semantic theories from earlier films. The language (the pictorial language, the images) is not enough to give a true, precise likeness of reality. One ought to construct a new language, says Juliette at one point in the film, the language being the house in which man lives. In *Two or Three Things* Godard contributes with a new style, an opportunity for change in seeing and communicating.

Godard lets his camera rest on Juliette and her girl-friend. On the red Austin which is gliding through a giant washing machine. On Juliette's husband who is talking to Juliette across the windscreen. On Juliette's car being cleaned. On the sun shining on the car, making it sparkle. On the figures of the dashboard. Are we convinced? Do we understand? Are we bored?

Godard gives as much attention to the things surrounding the characters of the story as to the characters themselves. They are shown up in all their expressiveness and beauty. The washed-down Austin could not be a more perfect advertisement for modern industry. There has not been such a beautiful poem written in praise of utility objects since Resnais' short film on plastic, *Le Chant du Styrène*. But more often the angle becomes more scornful, more drastic, as in Godard's ironic image of the modern service establishment: a combined brothel and crèche where the attendant wants payment in the form of tins. The French accent is underlined by the colour. Red, white and blue are dominant, and the play of colour often has an ironic effect.

The division of interest between men and things is valid, for in *Two or Three Things* Godard shows us people who allow themselves to be governed by things: man in the machine age. Juliette makes ' *amour a l'Italienne* ' for a Vogue dress or a coat by Paco Rabanne; Marianne, too, supplements her wardrobe through prostitution, and a 42-year-old woman testifies that she has lost her job — maybe to a computer? But there are revolutionaries too: an Algerian boy who is introduced as the hope of the twentieth century or a coloured couple making love in a dark basement — or more romantic characters like Paulette the little manicurist who talks about her work, her fiancé, her literary interests and her plans for the future in a happy home surrounded by children and books the most moving confession in the film.

Between the confessions are the director's own whispered meditations on the society he paints and the rules that govern his art. The commentary guides and gives stability to the rhapsodic episodes of the film. Sometimes the words are at odds with the pictured material — the people and the things — and out of this conflict Godard creates emotionally charged and sensually exciting experiences. He might for instance interrupt the objective description of the car-washing in the garage and paint his colour camera into the leafy branches of a tree, in a poetic side-stepping movement. The unexpected is always lying in wait behind the most concrete pictures, challenging our imagination and our feelings. The sudden shifts when logic and sobriety turn into pure seduction are very much part of the charm of the film and the secret of Godard's suggestiveness.

189

In *Two or Three Things* there is a sequence radiating an almost magical tension, a scene in which Godard is immersed in thought over a cup of espresso coffee. The whole ' scope screen is taken up with the surface view of the coffee in the cup and the bubbles rising from the sugar as it dissolves. The film disappears. The observed object takes possession of the screen. Fantastic winter streets and cosmic *motifs* are revealed within the shell of the blue cup. Or are we maybe seeing cells dividing themselves in rapid mutations? Microcosm and macrocosm in a fascinating synthesis.

INTERVIEW WITH ANNA KARINA BY ALISTAIR WHYTE (1973)

Anna Karina appeared in her first film at the age of fourteen. Three years later she left her native Denmark to work as a model in Paris where she met Jean-Luc Godard whom she was later to marry. In 1959 she played the leading feminine role in his second feature, *le petit soldat*, but the film ran into censorship difficulties and was banned for several years. By the time it was released Anna Karina had appeared in many other films and had emerged as one of the leading young actresses of the French cinema. Her partnership with Godard, which produced such films as *A Woman is a Woman*, *Live Your Life*, *Pierrot le fou*, etc., lasted until 1966, and since then she had worked with a number of distinguished directors including Luchino Visconti, Tony Richardson, George Cukor. In 1973 she produced, wrote and directed a feature film, *Vivre ensemble*, in which she takes the leading role. Inevitably, comparisons have been made with Jean-Luc Godard's films and the characters she played in them.

ALISTAIR WHYTE: Coming back to the character in the film, the character Julie, in many ways anyone who had seen some of the films you made with Godard might see similarities between this character and those you played in his films.

ANNA KARINA: I don't know if people feel that Julie in *Vivre ensemble* is similar to the female characters in Godard's pictures. I don't think so — the good thing about Jean-Luc's films is that the characters are very different every time. If you compare the heroine of *A Woman is a Woman* to the girl in *Live Your Life* or *Bande à part*, you see that they are really very different — or *Pierrot le fou* or *Made in USA* or *Alphaville*.

ALISTAIR WHYTE: When you look back at a film such as *A Woman is a Woman*, how do you feel? I believe you have seen the film again recently.

ANNA KARINA: When I see films I am in, I feel touched because I start to think about everything that was going on at the time — on the set, behind the set, with the people. I never really like myself

191

very much because I feel I could do much better now, but there is nothing you can do about it. I mean it's there, it's too late to cry. I feel moved when I look back, especially by Jean-Luc's pictures.

ALISTAIR WHYTE: Was your acting style moulded and developed by Jean-Luc Godard?

ANNA KARINA: My life was influenced by Jean-Luc because he taught me everything. I met him when I was very young and didn't know much about anything at all. He made me read, he showed me things. It was like a school, a very good school actually. I have seen his latest film, *Tout va bien*, three times, I liked it very much. I think it's again a picture people will like in ten years' time.

ALISTAIR WHYTE: Did he encourage you to consider a character as a whole? For example in something like *A Woman is a Woman*, were you asked to have an overall conception of the character you were playing or did you do it virtually from day to day?

ANNA KARINA: Jean-Luc never showed you a script. It's in his head, and it's as if you are doing a story every day which means that you really have to give everything every day. I mean, you give what he wants you to give.